noted 1-19-95

Low-Cost

Pole Building Construction

Low-Cost
Pole Building Construction

by
Doug Merrilees and Evelyn Loveday

Revised and Enlarged by
Ralph Wolfe

A Garden Way Publishing Book

 Storey Communications, Inc.
Pownal, Vermont 05261

Printed in the United States by Alpine Press
Ninth Printing, May, 1987

Library of Congress Cataloging in Publication Data

Merrilees, Doug.
   Low-cost pole building construction.

   Bibliography: p.
   Includes index.
   1. Building, Wooden.   2. Wooden frame houses.
3. Poles (Engineering)   I. Loveday, Evelyn V.,
joint author.   II. Wolfe, Ralph 1949-   III. Title.
TH1111.M47 1980   694   80-10232

ISBN 0-88266-170-1

Contents

III. Pole Building Plans   129

Tables

Hexagon house, Richard Owen Abbott. Detail at the corner.

Introduction

Would you hang your house between telephone poles? The idea is not as silly as it sounds. In fact, as some 600,000 owners of pole houses, barns, vacation cottages, and commercial buildings in the United States and Canada will attest, the idea is downright sensible. Pole building—a system of widely spaced poles embedded in the ground, supporting both roof and floor—is an easy-to-build, low-cost alternative to conventional building methods. The pole building system is easily adaptable to even the most difficult sites: steep hills, rocky soils, marshy or floodland areas, sandy beaches, hurricane or earthquake zones. And the system's simplicity places pole building within the scope of the weekend do-it-yourselfer or the eager but inexperienced novice.

Though received with skepticism when first introduced on the West Coast in the 1950s, pole buildings have earned the respect of the construction industry. In fact, properly constructed pole buildings, whether owner-built or contracted, can meet all FHA requirements to qualify for mortgage insurance under local review.

The pole building system has an elegant clarity. Large pressure-treated wooden poles are embedded in the ground, then linked at floor and roof levels with horizontal wood girders. Across these girders the floor and roof are laid; walls, windows, doors, and fixtures attached; and the house is a home!

Because there is no continuous concrete or block foundation, no excavation is necessary beyond digging the pole holes. The poles triple-function as foundation, structural frame, and wind bracing. Since the poles offer a rigid frame firmly anchored into the earth, the building is highly resistant to the wind forces of shear, racking, overturning, and uplift—forces that could flatten a lesser structure.

Labor, time, and materials are saved when building with poles. There's no waiting for the foundation to cure. Moreover, the roof can be built before floors and walls are completed, protecting workers and materials from the weather.

Pole buildings are simple enough to be assembled by unskilled workers. Less sawing is re-

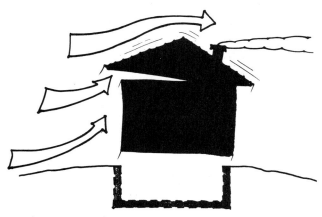

Wind forces on a building: Uplift.

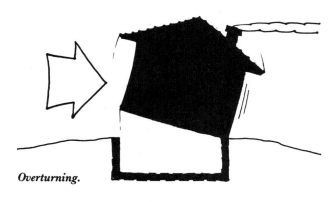

Overturning.

Racking.

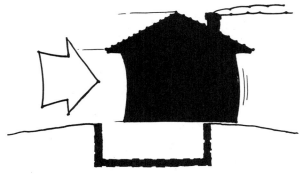

Shear.

quired than in conventional stud framing. No forms are needed. Since excavation and masonry work are minimized, foundation costs (15 percent in the typical house) are sharply reduced, and highly skilled subcontractors are not required. If the site is inaccessible or remote from roads and utility lines, the entire structure can be built with hand tools (although electricity will make sawing and drilling much less tedious).

The poles themselves may be round, like telephone poles, or squared off into timbers. Squared poles make joinery somewhat easier and reduce on-site construction time. But round poles are considerably cheaper, and 18 percent stronger than square poles of the same cross-sectional area. The reason for this extra strength is that knots and other defects in round poles remain "bound in" with the surrounding wood fibers, and contribute to the pole's resistance to bending. As a result, round poles of a lower lumber grade may be used to achieve the same strength as expensive, high-grade square poles.

Since the poles carry the roof's weight, the walls are not load bearing. They therefore may be less substantial than conventional stud walls, and may be built of cheaper-grade lumber. And since the walls have no roof-supporting responsibilities, they are independent of the structure above, and may be arranged as desired.

Pole construction has a further bonus: fire safety. Heavy timber structures are safer under fire conditions. In a severe fire, stud framing will burn quickly, like kindling in a fireplace. Even steel is not fire-safe: subjected to the intense heat of a fire, unprotected steel expands, distorts, and fails, collapsing the building with it. Widely spaced timbers, on the other hand, have the fortunate tendency to self-extinguish after forming a charred outer surface. The phenomenon is familiar to anyone who has tried in vain to set a single large log afire. This is not to say that a wooden pole building cannot burn down; it can, and will. But the pole structure affords an extra measure of safety, remaining in place and holding up the roof a little longer so that occupants can escape.

For this reason, pole buildings have been approved where light frame structures are prohibited because of fire hazard. Pole construction is

Rear view, MacDonald house. Edward J. Seibert, architect.

Photo by Von Guttenberg Photographic Studio

now recognized by all four U.S. model building codes.

Pole buildings can be constructed on steep hillsides where standard construction is infeasible or prohibitively expensive. Such "unbuildable" lots may be bought cheaply, and thus the total building cost drastically reduced. Little or no grading is required, so disturbance of the natural surroundings is minimized.

As inflation forces people to build more cheap-ly, it's easy to see why pole building has become so popular. Inexpensive site, cheaper materials, quicker completion time, and a reduced dependence on skilled labor all combine to make pole building an attractive alternative. According to Donald Patterson, structural engineer, "Construction experience has shown that building costs may be reduced by 25 to 50 percent or more by using pole-type design." And opportunities for building it yourself can cut costs even further.

Economics of Pole Construction

The costs of a pole building, and the opportunities for saving, depend upon whether you plan to hire a builder or build it yourself.

A conventional *contractor-built house* currently costs about $40 to $50 per square foot of living space.* This price includes labor (about 30 percent), materials (about 40 percent), and overhead and profit (about 30 percent).

The cost of construction can also be broken down another way, as follows: about 15 percent of it goes to build the basement foundation. Fifty percent is spent building the shell of the building. Another 15 percent is for plumbing, heating, and electricity. Kitchen cabinets, interior doors and trim, and hardwood floors account for another 15 percent, and 5 percent is miscellaneous expense.

The masonry work for the basement and foundation of an average house could cost around $10,000. A contractor-built pole foundation, on the other hand, will cost much less—perhaps one-third as much.

The contractor also will save some labor and materials in the framing and shell of the building, if familiar with pole construction. Of the $20,000 to $30,000 spent on the shell, perhaps $3,000 to $5,000 may be saved.

All other costs are similar to those of conventional construction. So the total estimated savings in building costs due to pole-frame construction is about 15 to 25 percent, or $10,000 to $20,000 on an average-sized house.

An *owner-built* pole house will be still cheaper: overhead and profit are eliminated, and labor costs are absorbed by the owner. But there are dis-economies. Materials will cost more without the contractor's discount at the lumberyard. Amateurs are slower workers, too. They make mistakes sometimes, and spend longer figuring

---

* All figures given are 1979 price estimates.

things out on the job. Nevertheless, it should be possible to build your own house, pole or otherwise, for half the cost of a contractor-built job.

The biggest saving with an owner-built pole house is in the foundation. Hand-digging is free if you do it yourself; hired labor will cost around $10 to $20 per six-foot hole. Or hire a backhoe with a 24-inch auger bit. Rates range from $300 to $500 per day, and the auger can dig a six-foot hole in about an hour. To the cost per pole of $40 to $90, add another $20 per pole for the labor costs of pole erection and alignment, footing and backfill, and the total costs range from $40 to $160 per pole. The foundation of a large house with sixteen poles would cost from $600 to $2,500, depending on how much of the work was done by hand.

Don't forget the considerable additional economy that can result when you build on an inex-

Facing page: The Smith house, another California pole house by Peter Calthorpe. Left: Pole playground structure in Waterfront Park, Boston.

pensive, "unbuildable" piece of land. Prime sites are very expensive; pole construction to utilize a hilly or marshy site can save thousands of dollars of the total cost of building a house.

Pole Building Designs

What kinds of buildings lend themselves to pole construction? The list is long and includes just about any type of commercial building, such as a warehouse or light manufacturing plant. Then there are farm buildings of all kinds—cow barns, horse barns, cattle sheds, poultry houses, tool sheds and the like. There are homes, too.

Prefabricated pole buildings for commercial and farm uses are obtainable from several manufacturers. The purpose of this book, however, is to show how you can do it yourself economically. Drawings and construction details for a variety of pole buildings, including houses, are pictured later in this book.

Word of Caution. Don't get the idea that construction of a pole house is an effortless weekend project. Any building, however simple, entails a lot of strenuous effort (one friend, muscling a bundle of shingles up onto the roof of his first pole house, confided his surprise at how *heavy* building materials turned out to be). The system is nonetheless easier and cheaper to build than conventional stud framing, and its conceptual simplicity is less intimidating to the novice. And as every do-it-yourselfer knows, the dirt and sweat wash off in the shower, leaving a rosy glow of satisfaction and pride at the sight of your own pole-frame castle, hand-built by owner.

I.

Pole Construction

First-year architecture students at Yale designed and built three cabins at a camp for urban kids in the countryside of Durham, Connecticut. One of the cabins is a pole building. Boxed photographs in chapter 7 outline the process followed by these first-time builders. Materials cost $4,000 in 1975. Construction plans can be found on page 157, if you'd like to try it yourself.

The photos, unless specifically credited, are by Patty Glazer.

1

History of
Pole Building

Pole building is an age-old type of construction that dates back to the Stone Age. A glance through Lloyd Kahn's *Shelter,* a fine compendium of traditional building types and technologies across the globe, reveals a nearly universal tendency to build houses on poles or stilts. In some areas, poles held houses high above flood plains, or provided a shady open-air ground floor for livestock or storage. In other climates, pole-frame construction afforded rigidity to withstand winter winds or heavy snows. Nomadic cultures favored the portability of light pole-frame dwellings.

Amos Rapoport in *House Form and Culture* says, "There are cases where a way of life may lead to . . . a dwelling form related to economic ac-

Yókuts Tule Lodges.

(Contributions to North American Ethnology, Vol. IV. Washington: U.S. Government Printing Office, 1881.)

Ho-de'-no-sote of the Seneca-Iroquois.   *Contributions to North American Ethnology.*

tivity rather than climate. For example, the Hidatsa of the Missouri Valley were agriculturists from April to November, growing corn, greens, and beans. During that period they lived in circular wooden houses thirty to forty feet in diameter with five-foot walls made of tree trunks and four central columns fourteen feet high supporting rafters carrying branches."

Rapoport goes on to comment on resistance to lateral forces, such as wind or earthquakes, that require either rigidity or bracing. "The Fiji Islands provide a number of examples of methods of dealing with the lateral force problem. In some areas the roofs are very simple and supported by central poles as well as peripheral columns. Since these poles are buried deep in the ground, the building acts as a rigid frame, although the flexibility of the members themselves assures some flexibility."

Traditional architecture in earthquake-prone Japan is classic pole construction: round poles at the corners of the building, supporting the heavy

Native Peruvian pole house.

The Isé shrine buildings in Japan use a traditional form of pole building construction.

roof and floor. The walls are lightweight panels of paper or wood. Pressure-treated, chemically preserved wood is not used; instead, the sacred temples such as the Isé Shrine are painstakingly rebuilt every twenty years by master craftsmen who precisely duplicate and replace every piece of wood in the building.

The modern use of treated poles in the construction of churches, schools, commercial buildings, vacation cottages, and houses began quite recently as a West Coast phenomenon, gaining impetus with the construction of the Marx Hyatt residence in Atherton, California. Modern methods were learned through the experience of utility and outdoor advertising companies. At the time there was resistance from both lending sources and building code reviewers, but since then enthusiasm for the many advantages of pole construction has burgeoned.

2

Attackers of Wood

Wood deteriorates because of bacteria, insects, fungi, and dampness. Fallen trees on the damp forest floor slowly rot; termites and fungi invade and consume old stumps and debris; the process is a vital, beneficial part of the self-sustaining ecology of the forest.

But when these scavengers encounter a tempting morsel in the form of a tasty new wooden house, the result may not be so benign. Anxious owners, concerned lest their pole house begin to disintegrate into the biosphere before its time, are well-advised to acquaint themselves with wood's natural enemies *before* they begin construction.

Fungus is the category of non-green plants which includes molds, yeasts, mushrooms, and mildew. They vary in size from a single cell to large parasitic organisms. The fungi that attack wood live on cellulose or lignin, breaking down the wood's structure until it becomes brittle and crumbles into powder (a condition known as *dry rot**). These organisms need oxygen, moisture, fa-

---

* Fungi will not attack dry wood (less than 20 percent moisture), hence the term *dry rot* is a misnomer.

vorable temperatures, and a food supply in order to thrive. Since the first three cannot be eliminated easily, preservatives are applied to the wood to eliminate the food supply.

Subterranean termites live in colonies in the ground, and are found throughout the United States except in the extreme northern reaches. Wood is the food of termites, and they will go to great lengths to get it. Since subterranean termites cannot survive exposure to open air and sunlight, they burrow up into wood which rests directly on or in the ground. If the wood is raised off the ground, these creatures will build mud shelter tubes up over foundation walls or other barriers, and infest the wood. Since they shun the light, termites may reveal no evidence of their infiltration until structural failures occur. Even dry wood is vulnerable, because subterranean termites can get water elsewhere.

Many builders in termite-prone areas recommend installation of termite shields as a barrier to infestation. Sheet metal aprons are placed along the top of the concrete foundation wall to block

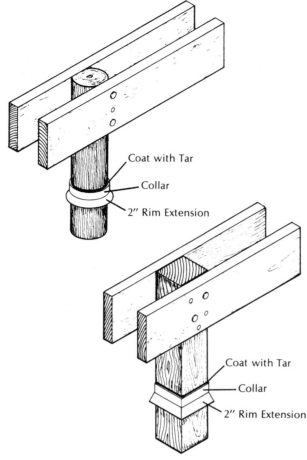

Coat with Tar

Collar

2″ Rim Extension

Coat with Tar

Collar

2″ Rim Extension

Termite shields have only limited effectiveness. They are no substitute for preservative-treated wood poles and lumber within eighteen inches of the ground.

the insect's passage into the wooden sill which rests upon it.

While termite shields may be somewhat helpful, it is a mistake to expect too much from them. Any gap, seam, or hole in the barrier renders the shield ineffective and allows termites to enter (a termite can penetrate a crack only 1/64-inch wide). And termite colonies have been known to build their mud tunnels up around the metal flanges intended to stop them.

Soil poisoning—the placement of poisons such as chlordane or heptachlor in the earth around the perimeter of the house—may be effective, but only temporarily. In time, the poison leaches away and the termites may return. And soil poisoning endangers the ground water, as well as pets and children playing around the house. Everyone knows that children eat dirt. Less well-known is the alarming increase in chemical con-

taminants that threatens to disrupt the nation's water supply. The Environmental Protection Agency predicts that by 1990, Massachusetts alone will suffer depleted water supplies in 155 of its 351 communities due to closed wells. For these reasons, soil poisoning is not a recommended defense against subterranean termites.

A better approach is to use wood pressure-treated with termite-repelling preservatives in all locations where wood comes close to or in contact with the ground, including wooden steps, handrails, trellises, and other wood within eighteen inches of the ground. Inspect pilings, poles, and footings regularly, and destroy mud tunnels if found. Use a sharp awl to probe wooden members for termite infestation. If evidence of damage is found, consult a termite specialist immediately. But prevention is the best cure; the extra cost of preservative-treated wood could be the best investment you'll ever make.

Flying termites are less widespread, occurring chiefly in the Southeast and Californian coastal regions, and in the Southwest (see map). They are much more difficult to locate and control, since they can enter a house through the walls, eaves, or roof. However, they do need contact with outside moisture. Homeowners in termite-infested areas of the country are doubtless familiar with neighbors' horror stories, and wise builders will take thorough precautions, such as using pressure-treated lumber inside and out, top to bottom.

Carpenter ants are distinguished from termites by their narrow waists (termites have full waists). They use wood primarily for nesting, rather than for food, so their damage is apt to be less widespread. Carpenter ants prefer soft or decayed wood; they can be deterred by pressure-treatment of the lumber.

Marine borers live in salt water, and will attack any wood between the water line and mud line. No species of wood is naturally immune. To protect against marine borers, choose poles that have been treated with a preservative that will not leach out in salt water.

Northern Limits of Termite Damage

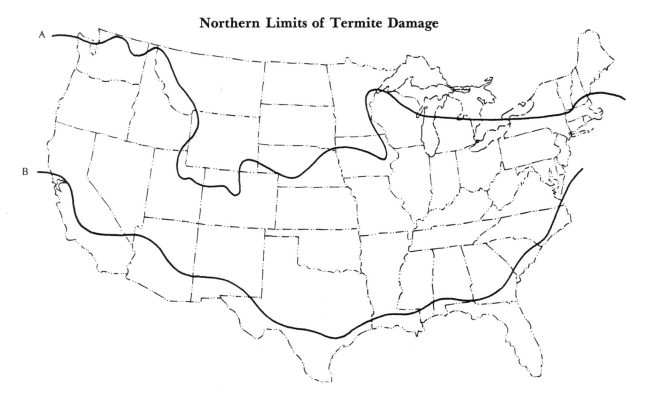

Limits of termite damage. **A.** *The northern limit of recorded damage done by subterranean termites in the United States;* **B.** *The northern limit of damage done by flying or nonsubterranean termites. Source:* Wood Handbook, *U.S. Department of Agriculture Handbook No. 72, 1955.*

Photo by George D. Walker

This pole was treated by Huxford Pole and Timber Company at their Huxford, Alabama plant. It is southern pine with a heavy penta treatment. Class 1, seventy feet long.

3

Preservative Treatments

In order to protect wood from its natural enemies, manufacturers have for seventy or eighty years been treating lumber with various preservatives. The bark is stripped, the pole is sprayed with fungicides, then pressure-impregnated with any of several chemicals. These toxic substances penetrate the wood's fibers, eliminating the food supply for fungi and insects.

How long will poles last before deteriorating? This is important, since the poles are the foundation and strength of the structure. A properly treated pole will last seven times as long as an untreated one, varying somewhat with species, treatment, and soil conditions. One manufacturer of treated poles says, "In the Thirties a well-treated pole was supposed to last thirty years. Now this estimate has risen to forty to fifty years, since anticipated failures did not occur. The length of service has been achieved under the most severe conditions. Of course, any pole which you use inside your building will be protected, and an even longer life can be expected."

The American Wood Preservers Institute (AWPI), conducting research for the Department of Housing and Urban Development, prepared the booklet *FHA Pole House Construction*, which sets forth guidelines acceptable to FHA for the construction of pole houses.

The AWPI is a non-profit organization doing research on pressure-treated woods of all kinds for all uses. Their comments on the durability of poles are especially valuable, although their standards are so high that not all manufacturers fully meet them.

AWPI says: "A house erected on poles produced for this purpose, and conforming to the rigid standards described below, is considered permanent—as permanent as a house on a well-constructed concrete foundation. The permanence is achieved by treating the poles with preservative. Using the newly perfected 'assay method,' pole manufacturers now can verify the adequate distribution of preservative in the finished product."

The assay testing method takes borings from the treated poles and subjects them to chemical analysis to determine the amount of preservative present.

AWPI goes on to say that "Users can be assured of the physical and preservative characteristics of the poles if the manufacturer indicates conformance with the AWPI quality control standards by the application of a permanent seal to each pole."

Preservative treatments vary widely in cleanliness, paintability, color, odor, and availability. In order to make a wise selection, first find out what types are available to you, and at what cost. Then choose the available treatment that most closely suits your needs.

Preservatives fall into two categories: oil- and gas-borne products, and water-borne products.

Oil-borne Products

Creosote, the original and best-known wood preservative, is made of distillates of tar and mixed petroleum oils. It is relatively insoluble in water, and has a strong odor and an oily surface which oozes at high temperatures. Wood treated with creosote is dark brown to black in color; painting is not possible, since creosote will bleed through the paint. It is highly toxic to organisms, and will kill plants in contact with it. Because of its toxicity, odor, and ooze, creosote should be used only on the exterior, and not for poles inside the house. Creosote is very common, and creosoted poles are readily available. Don't buy "landscaping timbers," which have been merely dipped into creosote. The penetration rarely exceeds ¼ inch, and the life of these timbers is very questionable.

Pentachlorophenol, or penta, is an organic compound applied in a 5 percent solution with light or heavy oil, or borne by gas. Penta is cleaner and easier to handle than creosote, and is every bit as toxic to insects, fungus, bacteria, animals, plants, and humans. It achieves good penetration, and is highly resistant to leaching. *Penta in heavy oil* leaves wood a light to dark brown color, with an oily surface. It has a long-lasting odor, and can't be painted until the oil evaporates (which could be months or more). Like creosote, penta in heavy oil oozes at high temperatures; like creosote, it is widely available. *Penta in light solvent* (mineral spirits) is comparatively clean, and usually paintable, provided the wood preserver knows prior to treatment that this is desired. It has a slight odor, and little effect on wood color. *Penta in a volatile petroleum solvent* (gas-borne) uses a gas such as propane or butane as a medium for pressure-treatment. The gas quickly disperses, leaving the penta locked in the wood. It is clean, paintable and odorless, and leaves the wood a natural color.*

Naphthenate solutions are oil solutions of copper or zinc naphthenate, usually applied by brush, sprayed, or dipped. *Copper naphthenate* is a good preservative, but it is bright green and hard to paint over. *Zinc naphthenate* is a less effective preservative, but easy to paint over. Both have a strong, persistent, objectionable odor.

Copper-8-Quinolinolate (solubilized) is odorless, and offers excellent decay resistance. And it is one

---

* Gray weathering is the result of fungi. Treated poles may not turn gray.

Recommended Preservatives and Retentions

Water-Borne Preservatives[1,2]   *Oil-Borne*[3]

	Chromated copper arsenate (CCA-Types A, B, C)	Ammoniacal copper arsenate (ACA)	Acid copper chromate (ACC)	Chromated zinc chloride (CZC)	Fluor chrome arsenate phenol (FCAP)	Pentachlorophenol[3]	Creosote & creosote-coal tar	AWPA Product Standards
AWPA Preservative Standard					**AWPA Standard**			
Product & Use					Minimum Net Retention in lbs./cu. ft.[4]			
Lumber and timber								
Above ground	0.25	0.25	0.25	0.46	0.22	0.40	8	C2
Soil or fresh water contact								
Non-structural	0.40	0.40	0.50	NR[5]	NR	0.50	10	C2
Structural-foundations,								
bridges, etc.	0.60	0.60	NR	NR	NR	0.60	12	C14
In salt water	2.5	2.5	NR	NR	NR	NR	25	C14
Plywood								
Above ground	0.25	0.25	0.25	0.46	0.22	0.40	8	C9
Soil or fresh water contact	0.40	0.40	0.50	NR	NR	0.50	10	C9
Piles								
Soil or fresh water use								
and foundations	0.80	0.80	NR	NR	NR	0.60	12	C3
In salt water								
Severe borer hazard—	2.5[8]	2.5[8]						
Limnoria[6]	&1.5	&1.5	NR	NR	NR	NR	NR	C18
Moderate borer hazard—								
Pholads[7]	NR	NR	NR	NR	NR	NR	20	C18
For both Pholads and								
Limnoria a dual treat-								
ment can be specified								
First treatment	1.0	1.0	NR	NR	NR	NR	—	C18
Second treatment	—	—	NR	NR	NR	NR	20	C18
Poles								
Utility								
Normal service conditions	0.60	0.60	NR	NR	NR	0.38	7.5	C4
Severe decay & termite areas	0.60	0.60	NR	NR	NR	0.45	9.0	C4
Building poles—structural	0.60	0.60	NR	NR	NR	0.45	9.0	C23

Source: Society of American Wood Preservers.

1 Trade names of water-borne preservatives: Chromated Copper Arsenate (CCA) (Type A); Greensalt, Langwood; (Type B) Boliden CCA; Koppers CCA-B; Osmose K-33; (Type C) Chrom-Ar-Cu (CAC); Osmose K-33 C; Wolman* CCA; Wolmanac CCA; Ammoniacal Copper Arsenate (ACA); Chemonite Acid Copper Chromate (ACC); Celcure Chromated Zinc Chloride (CZC); none Fluor Chrome Arsenate Phenol (FCAP); Osmosalts* (Osmosar*); Tanalith; Wolman FCAP; Wolman FMP.

2 Where cleanliness, paintability or odor are factors, and in certain salt-water areas, the approved water-borne preservatives should be used. Creosote, creosote-coal tar solution, and oil-borne penta are not recommended in these cases.

3 Penta in light or water-repellent solvents, and liquid petroleum gas carriers can provide clean, paintable surfaces. The processor should be advised when painting after treatment is intended.

4 AWPA Standard CI applies to all process and types of materials. Minimum net retentions in this chart conform to AWPA standards for all softwood species in the cases of lumber and plywood. Retentions for piles, poles and posts are based on AWPA Standards for southern pine. When other species are used for these items, AWPA requires different retentions. All water-borne retentions are oxide basis.

5 NR—Not recommended.

6 Limnoria Tripunctata are usually the most destructive marine borers. They are active over a wide geographic range, but most severe attack occurs in warmer waters up to 38°N latitude. Isolated severe Limnoria attack sometimes occurs above this latitude. Water-borne CCA and ACA are effective preservatives against Limnoria Tripunctata, Teredo and Bankia.

7 Pholads are usually less damaging than Limnoria and do most damage in warm Gulf Coast, Southern California and Southern Florida waters. Creosote-coal tar is effective against pholads.

8 The retentions are based on two assay zones—0 to 0.50 inch and 0.50 to 2.0 inches.

of the few effective preservatives that is not toxic or irritating to humans or animals. But it is not recommended for in-ground use.

Note: Preservative oils, creosote, and the liquid pentachlorophenol petroleum solutions used on poles sometimes travel from the treated wood along nails, and will discolor adjacent plaster or finished flooring. Oil types, however, have a maximum service life.

Water-borne Products

The water-borne preservatives leave wood clean to handle, odorless, and paintable. Some compounds will leach out, others won't. Leaching occurs faster in air than underground, surprisingly enough. For good results water-borne chemicals must be pressure-impregnated. Then the wood must be re-dried after treatment to remove excess moisture. All water-borne preservatives listed below are toxic to decay-causing fungus and bacteria and insects.

Acid Copper Chromate (ACC), sold under the brand name *Celcure,* is corrosive to metal. It is not recommended for in-ground use.

Ammoniacal Copper Arsenate (ACA) is very resistant to leaching, and is suitable for ground contact use. It will not bleed through concrete, plaster, or paint. ACA is sold under the brand name *Chemonite.*

Chromated Copper Arsenate (CCA types A, B, C) will not leach, and is suitable for in-ground or in-water use. It will not bleed through. CCA is available under a variety of names: *Greensalt, Langwood, Boliden CCA, Koppers CCA-B, Osmose K-33, Chrom-Ar-Cu (CAC), Osmose K-33C, Wolman CCA,* and *Erdalith,* among others.

Chromated Zinc Chloride (CZC) is reasonably toxic to decay-causing fungus and bacteria and insects, with the added bonus of good fire retardancy at high concentrations. But it resists leaching poorly, and is not recommended for ground contact. CZC is corrosive to metal fastenings.

Fluor-Chrome-Arsenate-Phenol (FCAP) is available as *Osmosalts, Osmosar, Tanalith, Wolman FCAP* and *Wolman FMP.* It is somewhat fire-retardant, and is non-corrosive. But it will leach out, so is not recommended for ground contact.

Hazards of Preservative Treatments

The chemical treatments used to preserve wood poles vary somewhat in odor, leachability, and toxicity to humans, but they are all poisons. This is unfortunately unavoidable: If a piece of wood is to survive being buried in the earth, it must be treated with poison to repel insects and decay. No poison is without hazard, and all must be handled with care. Make certain that the poles you purchase are clean and dry. Conscientious preserving plants steam-clean the treated wood, then let it season outdoors for sixty days before sale. Under these conditions, the chance of contamination is minimized, since very little of the preservative chemicals are likely to leave the wood once it is in place. In any case, be sure to wear gloves and protective clothing when handling treated wood, and do not burn treated wood scraps (the smoke may contain toxic vapors). Be very careful when using liquid preservative compounds for field-treatment, and keep them well away from children and pets.

The Environmental Protection Agency is currently examining the possible health hazards of creosote, pentachlorophenol and inorganic arsenic compounds such as CCA and ACA, the chemicals used to treat approximately 95 percent of all poles in the United States. These substances are suspected of being carcinogenic and mutagenic, and a full hearing is now under way to examine the evidence and to issue new regulations, if necessary. Because such decisions are often influenced by political forces, not even the insiders can hazard a guess about the outcome. The products could be cleared of all risk, they could be placed under stricter regulation (such as limiting their use to registered applicators who observe safety standards), or they could conceivably be banned altogether, forcing the industry to use alternative treatments.

Until the EPA issues its conclusions, creosote- and penta-treated products will continue to be available. Use them with proper caution, and consult your state Agriculture Department for the latest information and local regulations.

Paste Preservatives

Untreated poles and those treated with pressure-impregnated preservatives will benefit from supplementary ground-line treatment with a paste preservative such as *penta grease.* This is because most decay and insect attacks occur within the top twelve inches of soil. Treatment of poles in this vulnerable zone will extend the life of untreated wood poles to fifteen years or more; pressure-treated poles with a ground-line treatment should last much longer. Paste preserva-

tives are easy to apply, and the materials to treat nine poles will cost only about $30. Among the pastes showing the best results are *Osmoplastic* (Osmose Preserving Co., 980 Ellicott St., Buffalo, NY 14209) and *Pol-Nu* (Chapman Chemical Co., P.O. Box 9158, Memphis, TN 38109).

To apply the paste, first set the pole in place. Paste preservatives are very caustic, so wear protective clothing, goggles, and a breathing filter. Coat the pole thickly with the paste from eighteen inches below ground to three to six inches above. Then wrap the coated area with sheet plastic or plastic-backed kraft paper, and staple it to the pole. Now the pole may be embedded. If you are very diligent, you will reapply the paste every ten years to eliminate the worry of pole failures.

Penta grease also should be used for on-site treatment of wood end grain and for application to field cuts or bored holes in the preserved pole. It is applied thickly ($\frac{1}{4}$ to $\frac{1}{2}$ inch) everywhere the pole has been cut or notched. It can be caulked into the exterior angles of a wood joint to inhibit decay there.

Used poles come in all shapes and conditions. Check carefully for rot, termites, or structural defects.

4

Buying Poles

Poles are sold in a range of lengths and diameters. *Utility* poles are the longest, ranging in length from twenty-five to fifty-five or sixty feet in five-foot increments. *Building poles* are somewhat shorter and smaller. The circumference of a pole at its tip determines its *class:* poles are categorized in classes 1 to 10, with class 1 being the largest (twenty-seven-inch circumference, or 8½-inch diameter at the tip). Because the poles are tapered, the butt end will be considerably larger. The taper adds approximately ¼ inch of circumference for each foot of length; see the following table to estimate the butt diameter of a given pole. (Note that these dimensions indicate circumference, not diameter. This is because circumference is easier to measure. Divide this figure by 3.14 to find the diameter.)

If the pole is sixteen feet or less, a four- to five-inch tip (classes 7 to 10) is sufficient for most building purposes. If longer than sixteen feet, a pole with a five- to six-inch tip (classes 5 to 7) should be adequate. Poles should be purchased two to three feet longer than needed, to allow for error in digging the holes. The top may be cut off after the rafters are in place.

Poles up to a nine-inch diameter and thirty feet long are readily available and relatively cheap. Longer poles may cost more. One Boston supplier of southern pine, penta-treated utility poles in May 1979, quoted a price of $70 apiece for class 6 poles (5½-inch tip diameter) thirty feet long. Class 3 poles (7.3-inch tip) were $90 each for thirty-foot lengths.

As an alternative, consider buying used poles from a utility company or a wrecker. A New England wrecking company in May 1979, offered thirty-five foot poles with eight-inch tips (class 2) for $1.50 per foot, half the cost of new poles. These poles have been used for pilings, buildings, or utility poles, and vary considerably in quality and condition. Examine them closely for cracks and decay. If they are cut, examine the end grain to see how deeply the preservative treatment has penetrated the pole. If no short lengths are available, buy a long one and cut it into two—taking care to treat the exposed end cuts with penta grease before embedment.

Most used utility poles are branded with a code, enabling the buyer to identify the pole's class, length, species and preservative treatment.

Dimensions of Douglas Fir (Both Types)
and Southern Pine Poles
(based on a fiber stress of 8,000 psi)

Class	1	2	3	4	5	6	7	9	10
Minimum Circumference at Top (Inches)	27	25	23	21	19	17	15	15	12
Length of Pole (Feet)	Minimum Circumference at 6 Feet from Butt (Inches)								
20	31.0	29.0	27.0	25.0	23.0	**21.0**	19.5	17.5	14.0
25	33.5	31.5	29.5	27.5	25.5	**23.0**	21.5	19.5	15.0
30	36.5	**34.0**	**32.0**	29.5	27.5	25.0	23.5	20.5	
35	39.0	**36.5**	**34.0**	**31.5**	29.0	27.0	25.0		
40	**41.0**	38.5	**36.0**	33.5	**31.0**	**28.5**	26.5		
45	**43.0**	**40.5**	37.5	**35.0**	**32.5**	30.0	28.0		
50	**45.0**	**42.0**	**39.0**	36.5	34.0	31.5	29.0		
55	**46.5**	43.5	**40.5**	38.0	35.0	32.5			
60	**48.0**	**45.0**	**42.0**	39.0	36.0	33.5			
65	49.5	**46.5**	43.5	40.5	37.5				
70	51.0	**48.0**	**45.0**	41.5	38.5				
75	52.5	49.0	**46.0**	43.0					
80	**54.0**	50.5	47.0	44.0					
85	55.0	51.5	48.0						
90	56.0	53.0	49.0						
95	57.0	**54.0**	50.0						
100	58.5	55.0	51.0						
105	59.5	56.0	52.0						
110	**60.5**	57.0	53.0						
115	61.5	58.0							
120	62.5	59.0							
125	63.5	59.5							

Patterson, Donald. Pole Building Design. *McLean, Virginia: AWPI, 1969.*

Note: Preferred standard sizes are those listed in boldface type. Those shown in light type are included for engineering purposes only.

Choose poles carefully. You'll soon find that poles come in all shapes—all except straight, that is.

To economize even further, you may be able to take your own trees to be pressure-treated, if there is a plant nearby. Softwoods like Douglas fir, southern pine, or hemlock are better than hardwoods, since they accept the preservative better, and are easier to nail or saw. Woods listed as approved for poles to be treated include western larch, southern yellow pine, Pacific Coast Douglas fir, lodgepole pine, jack pine, red or Norway pine, Ponderosa pine, western red cedar, and northern white cedar. White pine also is used in the East, as are white and red spruce.

However, if you have ready access to white or red cedar, locust, redwood heart, or cypress, the poles made from these woods will be inherently more resistant to rot and microorganisms. Hemlock also is rot-resistant but is more often used as lumber. For longest life, these woods should still be pressure-treated, especially in damp or termite-prone areas.

Bear in mind that transporting the poles may be more expensive than the poles themselves. They are very heavy, and will require a flatbed truck, a block and tackle, and several strong pole-wrestling friends.

To avoid the cost of pressure-treated poles, you may think of treating them yourself. We advise you not to. Home treatment of poles is inadequate and dangerous. The preservatives cannot penetrate far enough to protect the wood sufficiently and the chemicals are poisonous. Since the poles are the most important structural member of your house, they should be pressure-impregnated to insure the greatest durability.

Pole construction is ideal for seaside sites.

5

Choosing a Site

Pole buildings can be built nearly anywhere, but some sites are obviously better than others. The optimum site will have a slight slope, just enough to allow good drainage.

Consider the general soil condition.

● *Below average soil* consists of soft clay, poorly compacted sand, clays containing large amounts of silt (with standing water during a wet period).

● *Average soil* includes loose gravel, medium clay or any more compact composition.

● *Good soil* includes compact, well-graded sand and gravel, hard clay, or graded fine and coarse sand.

Sandy gravel is best for drainage; try to avoid sites with heavy, wet clay soil and low land with a high water table.

From an energy conservation standpoint, the best site is one with a good southern exposure, but well-protected against icy winter winds (usually from the north). Valley bottoms are cold in the winter; so are exposed hilltops. Shade trees east and west of the house will block much of the summer sun. Ask the local National Weather Service office for prevailing wind directions in summer and winter, and plan your house site accordingly, for maximum comfort at minimum cost.

Hillside sites require different building techniques. On steep slopes, a concrete *keywall* may be used as an anchor on the uphill side. In this case, the floor acts as a structural membrane, tying the other poles to the keywall. So the floor must be sturdy, sound, and continuous. It may be prudent to consult an engineer or architect for advice before building on a difficult site; the small expense could prevent a big disaster.

Determine the possibility of slides (again, ask an engineer if you are unsure). On a hillside site, it is vital to provide proper drainage in order to protect the natural vegetation and to prevent erosion and loss of pole anchorage. Wherever possible, excavate by hand to avoid damage caused by bulldozers, backhoes, and tractors. The plants and roots thus saved will help hold together the fragile fabric of topsoil. If necessary, dig *rain*

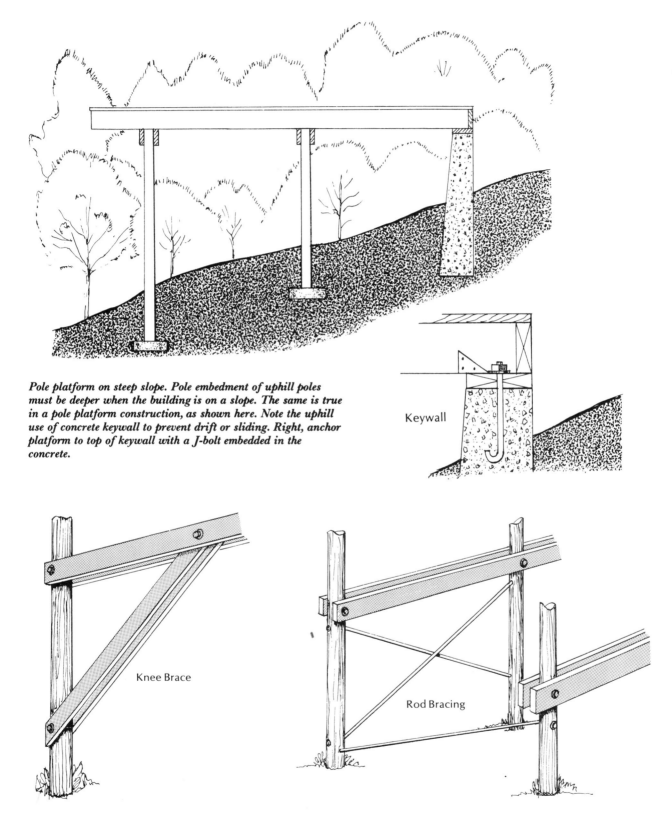

Pole platform on steep slope. Pole embedment of uphill poles must be deeper when the building is on a slope. The same is true in a pole platform construction, as shown here. Note the uphill use of concrete keywall to prevent drift or sliding. Right, anchor platform to top of keywall with a J-bolt embedded in the concrete.

Keywall

Knee Brace

Rod Bracing

If poles cannot be embedded to recommended depth, some form of **wind bracing** *is recommended. Shown are two alternatives.*

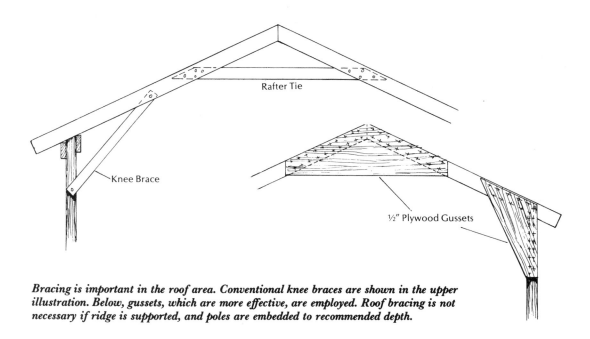

Bracing is important in the roof area. Conventional knee braces are shown in the upper illustration. Below, gussets, which are more effective, are employed. Roof bracing is not necessary if ridge is supported, and poles are embedded to recommended depth.

leaders—shallow trenches to divert surface drainage away from the house.

Rocky sites offer advantages—and disadvantages. Embedment depth may be reduced if the poles sit on bedrock, since frost heaves pose no problem. But the poles may not be embedded deep enough to resist lateral loads from the wind.

With adequate cross-bracing, the poles need only be embedded deep enough to prevent drift and slippage (about four feet in most soils). If the rock ledge is encountered less than four feet down, a pole seat at least three inches deep should be made in the rock to hold the butt secure. The house frame can be cross-braced with ⅝- or ¾-inch threaded steel rod, in drilled holes flooded with preservative. Only a few such rods are needed, because of the steel's great strength. As an alternative, wood knee-braces can be installed under the floor. Shear walls (rigid rectangular wall panels running in two directions) also can serve as cross-bracing. A utility room sheathed inside and out with ⅝-inch plywood, and firmly attached to the building frame, will do the trick. Sturdy connections are crucial. Try to picture your house straining under hurricane-force winds, and you will understand the necessity for such precautions.

Interior of Camp Cabin 1, showing the boxed-in corners and open shutters.

6

Choosing a Design

The pole building you construct may be as simple or elaborate as you desire. The choice of design will depend upon your current and future need for space, and upon the money available. If you plan to build it yourself, the project also will depend upon your level of building skill and experience, your enthusiasm, and the amount of time you have available for construction. Assess these factors carefully as you choose your pole building project.

If you have some knowledge of carpentry, the construction tips and illustrated examples should provide you with plenty of ideas. Feel free to mix and match from the several approaches included here as you develop a plan of your own. The general process of construction is outlined in the following pages, along with tables to help you choose appropriate lumber sizes as you design.

If you are a novice and wary of your ability to improvise, you may prefer to build according to one of the designs included in the back of this book. These plans are all relatively simple, and offer a range of building types and sizes to suit various needs and budgets.

If you are a rank beginner, you will need to do a little homework before putting saw to lumber for the first time. Carpentry and construction are not really so difficult, even for the neophyte. But it is beyond the scope of this book to provide detailed explanations of the use of tools, staircase construction, chimney flashing, window details, and so forth. Refer to the Bibliography for a list of construction textbooks; these should help fill in gaps in your building skills.

Those who are short on time or inclination may decide to hire a builder for the job. Discuss your ideas with a reliable contractor or local architect, preferably one familiar with pole building. They'll be able to translate your sketches into a building.

There are two categories of pole buildings: those with a full pole frame, and those that use the poles to support a platform for a conventional frame structure. Both approaches make use of an easy and inexpensive pole foundation system suitable for hilly or difficult sites. The *platform* method permits the builder to use conventional construction techniques, and may be preferred

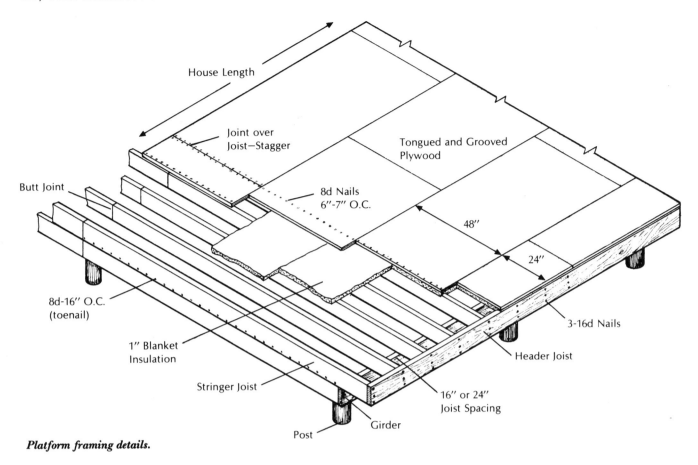

House Length

Joint over
Joist—Stagger

Tongued and Grooved
Plywood

Butt Joint

8d Nails
6″-7″ O.C.

48″

24″

8d-16″ O.C.
(toenail)

3-16d Nails

1″ Blanket
Insulation

Header Joist

Stringer Joist

16″ or 24″
Joist Spacing

Post

Girder

Platform framing details.

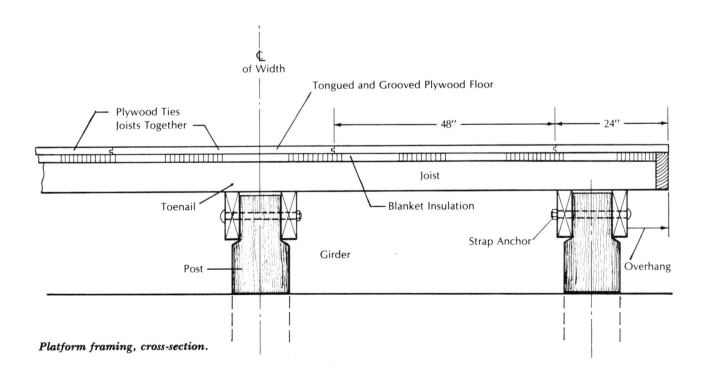

₵
of Width

Tongued and Grooved Plywood Floor

Plywood Ties
Joists Together

48″

24″

Joist

Toenail

Blanket Insulation

Strap Anchor

Post

Girder

Overhang

Platform framing, cross-section.

by a contractor unfamiliar with pole construction. For this reason, it may be cheaper. But the full *pole frame* building affords greater strength and lateral resistance to the forces of wind, flood, and earthquake. As an additional advantage, the roof can go up first, sheltering subsequent work. For do-it-yourselfers, pole frame construction should be less expensive.

Make sure that your pole building design is appropriate to the site. In addition to the energy conservation factors discussed earlier, consider these: Which direction affords the best view? From what direction will cars and people approach? Where should the main entrance be? Will there be an attached garage? Where will the driveway run? How close to the property line am I legally allowed to build? Shall I plan for morning sun in the bedrooms, afternoon sun in the living room? Is the kitchen conveniently close to the parking area for grocery unloading? Where will garbage be kept? Are the windows arranged to permit easy supervision of children's outside play from the kitchen or living areas? Where will gardening and yard equipment be stored? Will there be a sunny area for the garden, a shady spot for summer lounging, a screened porch for the bug season? How about a mud room or vestibule for winter clothing and sports equipment?

Other considerations include the shape of the house. Because floors are cheaper to construct than roofs, a multi-story building is somewhat more economical than a single-story building of the same floor area. Compared to a ranch house, the multi-story dwelling also will conserve energy because of its more compact shape. Fewer poles are required—each does double duty—and fewer holes need to be dug. But a multi-story house may be more difficult to build: the poles are longer and heavier. Taller ladders and scaffolding are required. A staircase must be built. In a very small house, the additional space required for the staircase may cancel the economy of multi-story construction. And a multi-story house presents a taller face to the winter wind: in cold, windy climates it will cost more to heat than a low house protected by surrounding trees.

Whatever type of building you decide upon, it

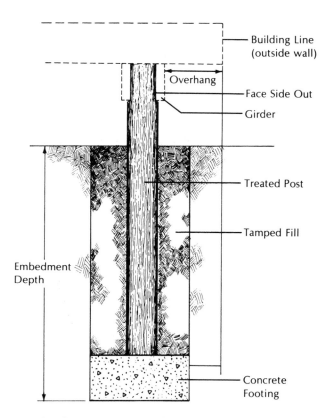

Details of platform construction. Joists may cantilever out as far as one-half their span with no increase in their size.

is a good idea to draw it carefully to scale as you design, examining on paper the construction details before you start to build. You'll save a lot of time, and avoid costly mistakes.

Use the drawings at the back of this book as a guide. Drawings like these make it much easier to calculate building dimensions and materials so as to avoid waste or shortage.

Use the tables on pages 83–85 to determine the safe sizes for structural lumber in your design. Lumber is most economical in lengths of fourteen feet or less. You pay a premium for lumber more than twenty feet long, and it is not readily available longer than twenty-four feet. So plan accordingly.

Take advantage of the *cantilever principle:* when joists or rafters are continuous, they may cantilever out beyond the girders as much as one-half their span, with no increase in joist size. Remember, though, that the girders are then carrying

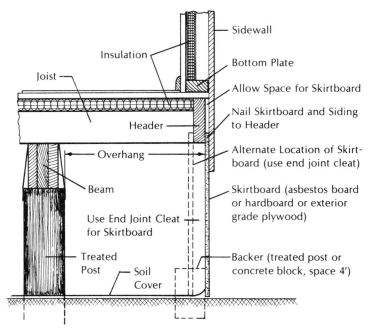

Section through side wall.

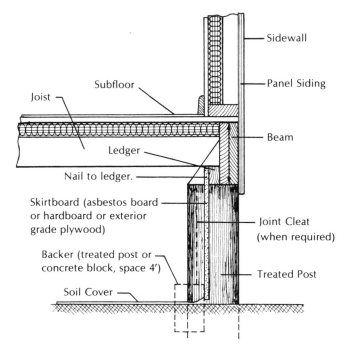

Section through side wall.

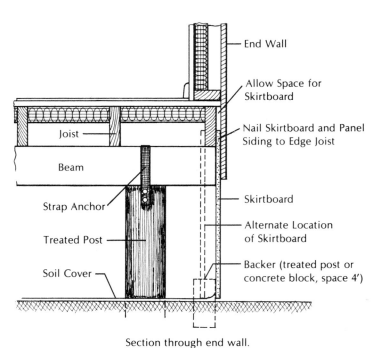

Section through end wall.

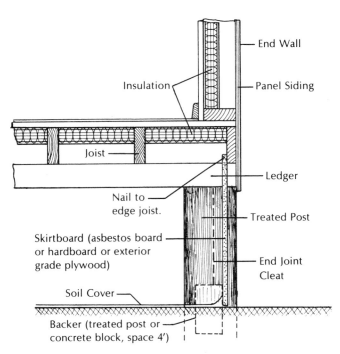

Section through end wall.

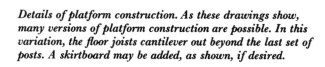

Details of platform construction. As these drawings show, many versions of platform construction are possible. In this variation, the floor joists cantilever out beyond the last set of posts. A skirtboard may be added, as shown, if desired.

Details of platform construction. In this version, skirtboard may be installed later, as shown.

more weight, and must be sized according to Table 5 in order to carry the cantilever above.

As you design your pole building, give some thought to the relationship between the poles and the exterior walls. In the simpler designs in this book, the poles are shown incorporated into the walls. This is the easiest system to build, using horizontal girts attached to the poles to support exterior siding. This approach has limitations, however: because the poles are never perfectly straight, the attached walls may wiggle unless small shims of wood are inserted to correct the imperfections. Shimming out the poles may be tedious if the building is large or the poles very irregular. Furthermore, it may be difficult to seal the joint between the siding and the pole to prevent costly heat leaks. Similar joint problems on the interior side of the wall complicate installation of wallboard or paneling. For these reasons, the pole-in-wall system is most appropriate for simple uninsulated barns and storage buildings, and for modest cottages in very warm climates.

These problems may be avoided by separating the poles from the wall. Place the poles either inside or outside of the enclosure. With the poles *outside*, weather-sealing is much simpler, since the shell of the house is nowhere penetrated by the poles. The poles themselves may be treated with creosote or other chemicals which, for reasons of odor or toxicity, could not be used inside the house.

If poles are treated with a more benign preservative, they may be placed *inside* the house. This allows the builder to conceal the poles if a more conventional external appearance is desired. The poles may be incorporated into interior walls (posing the same alignment problems mentioned before), boxed in with wallboard, or left as freestanding columns in the house. Such columns may be used to architectural advantage (see the design for the Solar Pole Cottage, page 167). Plan them carefully to avoid difficulties where the columns must penetrate ceilings, floors or cabinetry, or where they may interfere with easy circulation or furniture placement.

The poles-inside system offers a major economy: because of the cantilever principle, the floor

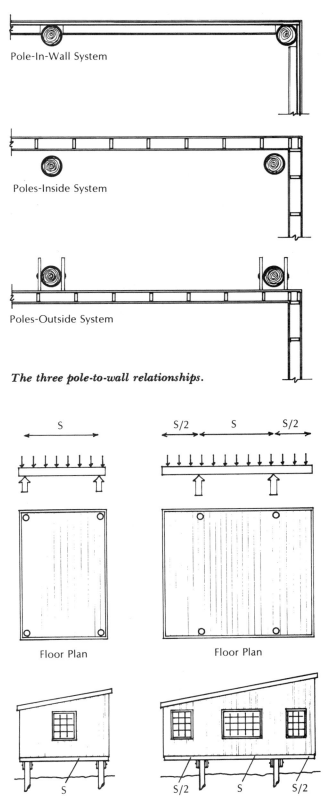

Pole-In-Wall System

Poles-Inside System

Poles-Outside System

The three pole-to-wall relationships.

Floor Plan

Floor Plan

Cantilevered joists or rafters may extend out as much as one-half the span with no increase in joist size, allowing a larger building to be built on the same pole foundation. Remember, though, that the supporting girders must be stronger to carry the larger weight on the joists above.

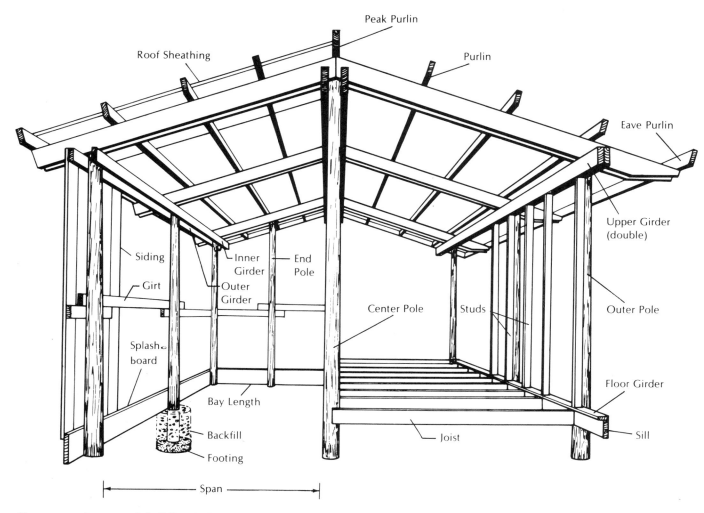

Two ways to frame a pole building. Left side of this cutaway view shows embedment of poles, attachment of upper girders, rafters, purlins and roof sheathing. Below are the splashboards, girts and siding. The right side is for a more finished building with a suspended floor, as indicated by floor girder and joists and wall framing inside the poles. Eaves are given more overhang. Purlins may be replaced by roof decking, or by adding more rafters every sixteen or twenty-four inches.

and roof may extend out beyond the poles which support them, providing a larger house for the same pole foundation. To put it another way: a house with poles inside, using the cantilever principle, requires fewer poles, holes, girders and connections than a comparable house with the poles outside the walls. The saving from this structural efficiency is substantial.

Whichever system you choose, plan your design for ease of construction. Remember that gypsum wallboard, interior paneling, and exterior plywood sheathing come in four-by-eight-foot sheets. If you plan to use these materials, try to design the building according to this four-foot module wherever possible, to avoid excessive cutting and patching.

Labor, Time, and Power

It is difficult to accurately estimate how long it will take to complete your pole building. Much depends on the number, skill, and speed of the workers, the weather, the size of the project, the availability of electricity, and so forth. Two enthusiastic amateur builders should be able to construct the Storage Shed, page 141, in about a week. The Small Barn, page 131, might take the same crew about three weeks. The more elaborate houses may take three months or more to complete.

For most aspects of construction, two persons make a good team: one cuts while the other nails. It is possible to build alone, although some jobs are difficult. A sixteen-foot 2×12 rafter weighs about 80 pounds, and may be tough to muscle up onto the roof and hold in place while you nail it yourself. Other jobs like measuring, using plumb bobs, and wielding plywood, also go better with two.

There are times when you'll want to ask for additional help, too: to unload the lumber truck when it arrives with two tons of lumber, and to help erect the poles. A twenty-foot pole weighs 500 to 1000 pounds; two workers cannot maneuver it into place without friends or a block and tackle. On the other hand, two persons shouldn't have too much trouble with a twelve-foot pole for a smaller building.

If you are going to bolt the girders to the poles or pre-bore nail holes, a temporary power source will be helpful. This will allow you to use an electric drill and later, in the sheathing work, a circular saw. If the building will not have electric service, of course both jobs can be accomplished with

Poles are heavy. Invite some friends over for the day. Buy some beer and work gloves.

hand tools. Hand-boring the poles for the roof girders is difficult, and even more arduous when working from a ladder rather than scaffolding. A gasoline-powered remote generator could be used to power tools when needed. If you anticipate adding a wind-electric generator in the future, make sure to choose an auxiliary gasoline generator with remote-start capability, so that it can become part of your eventual wind energy system. (For further information, see *Home Energy for the Eighties,* by Ralph Wolfe and Peter Clegg.)

Detail showing roof framing and girders splice.

7

The Fastenings
to Use

Carpenters use nails as fasteners in conventional stud frame construction, because they are cheap and easy to put in place, and because the structure is redundant enough to remain safe if a few nails fail to hold.

Pole frame buildings, on the other hand, rely on a few stout members and a few solid joints to carry the weight of the structure. The connections *must* be secure, solid, and permanent. Buildings flex in the wind; wood shrinks and swells with the seasons; unprotected steel rusts; and joints suffer the consequences. Make sure that your pole frame connections are equal to their tasks.

Nails or Bolts. There is no difference in *shearing* strength among nails, bolts, lag screws, or spikes of the same diameter. But there is considerable difference in the capacity to resist withdrawal. Nails and spikes can be pulled out, or can work loose if the building flexes in the wind. This flexure may be almost unnoticeable to occupants, but over the years the spike may gradually be worked out of its hole. Sometimes the seasonal shrinkage and swelling of the wood will do the

same thing. To protect against spikes working loose, use cement-coated spikes or *barn spikes,* which have a screw-like shank. Use threaded nails for lesser jobs.

The choice of fasteners lies primarily in which is easier for you. Lead holes should be drilled for spikes, particularly near the ends of planks, to prevent splitting. This can be done on the ground, whereas holes for bolts that go through the poles must be drilled after the poles have been erected.

For the strongest possible connection of girder to pole, use a *spike grid.* This may be curved on one side, for joining a round post to a flat girder. It adds considerable strength to the joint. Use a high-strength threaded rod to squeeze the grid spikes into the wood, then replace it with a galvanized bolt.

Another strong joint may be obtained by *dapping* the pole: notching out a flat area for better contact with the girder. Dapping also provides a little ledge which carries some of the vertical load. Remember that any cut or notch must be treated with preservative in the field.

The accompanying table lists recommended

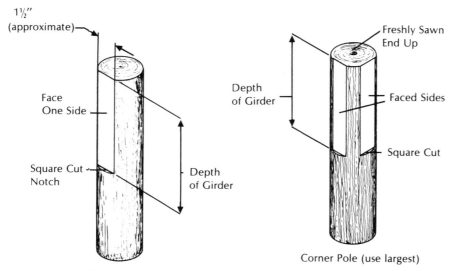

1½″ (approximate)

Face One Side

Square Cut Notch

Depth of Girder

Freshly Sawn End Up

Depth of Girder

Faced Sides

Square Cut

Corner Pole (use largest)

For a stronger joint, **dap the poles** *for better contact with the girder.*

nail sizes for various construction joints. The sizes are listed by penny number or "d"; the chart translates these into inch lengths. Galvanized nails should be used wherever rusting may occur. They also hold better than uncoated nails.

The following pages illustrate a variety of manufactured metal fastening devices developed by Teco (5530 Wisconsin Ave., Washington, D.C.

20015). Such fasteners often simplify construction, save time, and in some cases save on materials. For instance, by using joist hangers rather than nailing the joists to the top of the girders, the total height of the wall will be reduced by the width of the joist. Other devices can provide supplementary or additional strength in joining rafters to girders or in tying across the ridge.

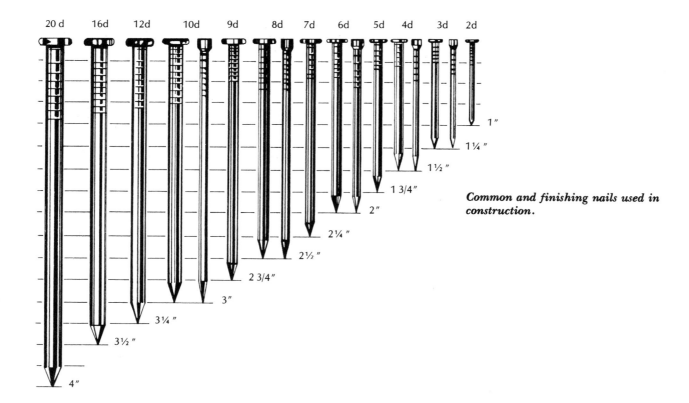

20 d   16 d   12 d   10 d   9 d   8 d   7 d   6 d   5 d   4 d   3 d   2 d

1″
1¼″
1½″
1 3/4″
2″
2¼″
2½″
2 3/4″
3″
3¼″
3½″
4″

Common and finishing nails used in construction.

Recommended Nail Sizes

Joining	Nailing Method	Nails Number	Size	Placement
Header to joist	End-nail	3	16d	
Joist to sill or girder	Toenail	2-3	10d or 8d	
Header and stringer joist to sill	Toenail		10d	16 inches on center.
Bridging to joist	Toenail each end	2	8d	
Ledger strip to beam, 2 inches thick		3	16d	At each joist.
Subfloor, boards:				
1 by 6 inches and smaller		2	8d	To each joist.
1 by 8 inches		3	8d	To each joist.
Subfloor, plywood:				
At edges			8d	6 inches on center.
At intermediate joists			8d	8 inches on center.
Subfloor (2 by 6 inches, T&G) to joist or girder	Blind-nail (casing) and face-nail	2	16d	
Soleplate to stud, horizontal assembly	End-nail	2	16d	At each stud.
Top plate to stud	End-nail	2	16d	
Stud to soleplate	Toenail	4	8d	
Soleplate to joist or blocking	Face-nail		16d	16 inches on center.
Doubled studs	Face-nail, stagger		10d	16 inches on center.
End stud of intersecting wall to exterior wall stud	Face-nail		16d	16 inches on center.
Upper top plate to lower top plate	Face-nail		16d	16 inches on center.
Upper top plate, laps and intersections	Face-nail	2	16d	
Continuous header, 2 pieces, each edge			12d	12 inches on center.
Ceiling joist to top wall plates	Toenail	3	8d	
Ceiling joist laps at partition	Face-nail	4	16d	
Rafter to top plate	Toenail	2	8d	
Rafter to ceiling joist	Face-nail	5	10d	
Rafter to valley or hip rafter	Toenail	3	10d	
Ridge board to rafter	End-nail	3	10d	
Rafter to rafter through ridge board	{ Toenail	4	8d	
	{ Edge-nail	1	10d	
Collar beam to rafter:				
2-inch member	Face-nail	2	12d	
1-inch member	Face-nail	3	8d	
1-inch diagonal let-in brace to each stud and plate (4 nails at top)		2	8d	

* 3 inch edge and 6 inch intermediate.

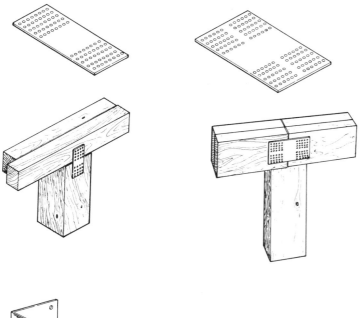

Flat Plate Connector. This device is especially useful for splicing beams together or for joining a flat beam to a round post in a top load situation.

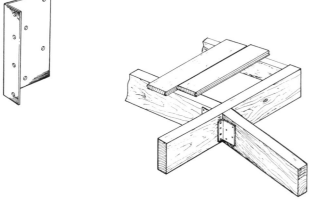

Angles. These fasteners come in many variations and are very handy for joining rafters to beams and to the ridge.

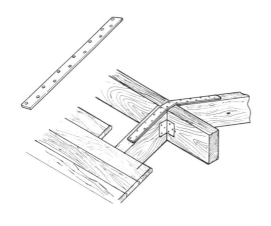

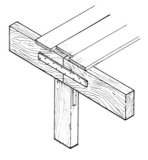

Strap Tie. This simple metal strap is perhaps the most versatile fastener and may be used for connecting many types of framing joints. Use it to tie down the roof to the building frame, to protect against damage from wind uplift.

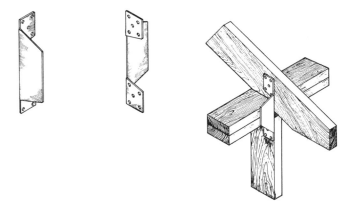

Rafter Anchor. These are used to anchor the building's rafters to the wall studs and also have application as tie-down devices.

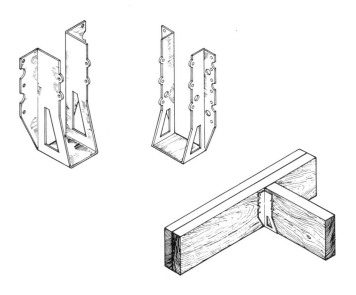

Joist and Beam Anchor. Use this bracket to hang joists between floor girders. It is available in sizes to fit most dimensions of lumber.

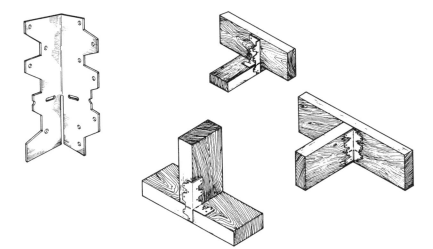

All-Purpose Framing Anchor. This fastener, like the strap tie, may be used in a number of applications, such as attaching joists to plates and roof trusses to plates.

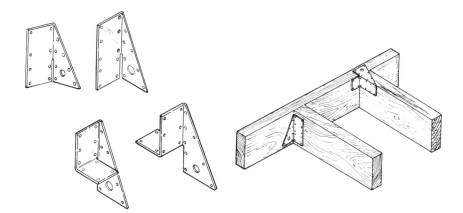

Triple Grip Framing Anchor. This device is used in the same applications as the all-purpose framing anchor, but it provides one additional nailing surface.

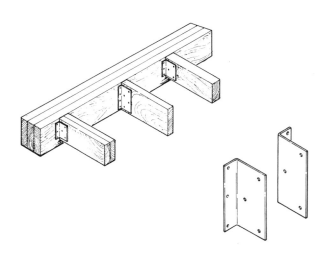

Anchor. This is a variation of the all-purpose framing anchor, and might be used in attaching floor joists (as shown) to sills.

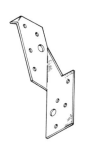
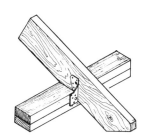

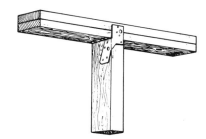

Dual Clip Framing Anchor. This fastener is similar to several other framing anchors but should be used for light loads and for shorter spans.

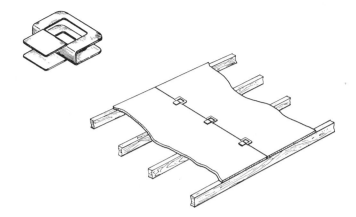

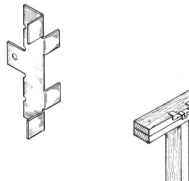

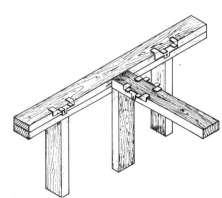

Plywood Supports. These fasteners are especially time-saving for leveling plywood. Their use eliminates the need for blocking at the joints.

Backup Clip. In a similar way to the supports this device provides a support for dry wall construction or paneling at the wall corners and ceiling joints.

8

The Process
of Construction

Begin by assembling all tools and structural lumber materials at the building site. A list of appropriate tools will be found in the Appendix. Store the lumber up on blocks to keep if off the ground, support it well to prevent warpage or sagging, and cover it from the weather. If rain is anticipated, order the lumber shortly before it will be used, so that it is not exposed to excessive moisture at the site. Gypsum wallboard, insulation, and flooring must be kept dry; do not order them until the building is enclosed.

The next step is to lay out the building according to the design you've chosen. First, roughly locate the corners of the building, using a tape measure. Construct batter boards around the corners as shown in the diagram on page 49. These boards should all be at the same level, placed a few feet beyond the corners to allow room for digging. Run strings between the batter boards to outline the building.

Square the corners with care by measuring the diagonals (which should be equal), or by measuring off a "builder's triangle" with sides of six, eight, and ten feet, or any multiples of three, four, and five. These string guidelines serve to locate the holes for the outer poles. Drop a plumb line from each intersection to locate the exact spot for the hole. When these are marked, the guidelines can be removed so they won't be in the way of digging. They can be replaced later to check the holes if you've marked their position on the batter boards.

In working with any pole plans it is difficult to control the building's precise dimensions on the basis of distances from center to center of the poles. This is because the poles vary in straightness, and also may vary in diameter. And it is difficult to dig a hole with precision. But do the best you can, and try to correct each inaccuracy in subsequent steps. Plywood is square, and if the building is not, it may be difficult to nail the plywood to the joists.

Planning and Digging the Holes

The depth of the holes will depend on the soil conditions, slope of the site, and the frost line. Poles on a level site in average soil should be embedded *at least* four feet (five feet if the eaves are to be higher than ten feet above the ground). Consult the following tables for a more specific recommendation.

Whatever the recommended embedment depth, make sure to dig below the frost line. The maps indicate approximate frostline depths in the United States. Use the map of Average Depth if your site has average conditions. For a wind-swept hill where the snow never accumulates, the frost line will be deeper; use the map of Maximum Depth. Ask a local farmer, builder, or architect to confirm this depth.

Hand digging is recommended, as it causes the least damage to roots and topsoil, which in turn helps hold the earth together around your pole. A post-hole digger is a must for this job; borrow or rent one. If you can't face digging twelve holes yourself, hire a local laborer or two. If absolutely necessary, the holes may be dug—carefully—by machine. Look for a contractor who specializes in pole buildings or sign erection.

Poles taper, and you will set the larger or butt ends in the ground. Dig holes six to eight inches larger in diameter than the butt of the pole. If the holes are of any considerable depth, however, they will have to be wider than that to allow digging room, unless a power auger or pole shovels are used, and also to allow for a concrete footing pad. A twenty-four-inch diameter earth auger will dig a neat hole with enough clearance to plumb and position the poles.

Beryl starts a hole for the poles. Hand-digging causes much less damage to the topsoil and vegetation than machine-digging, and saves money.

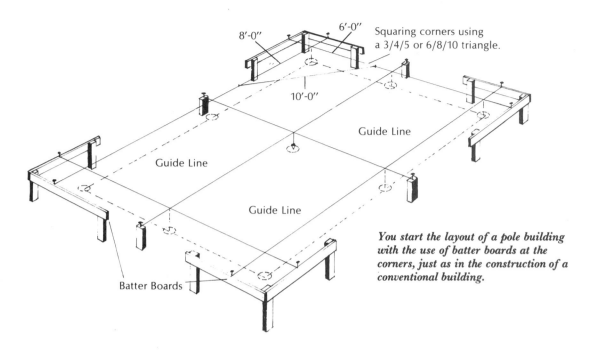

8'-0" 6'-0" Squaring corners using
a 3/4/5 or 6/8/10 triangle.

10'-0"

Guide Line

Guide Line

Guide Line

Batter Boards

You start the layout of a pole building with the use of batter boards at the corners, just as in the construction of a conventional building.

A crew of energetic friends makes hole-digging quicker and much more pleasant.

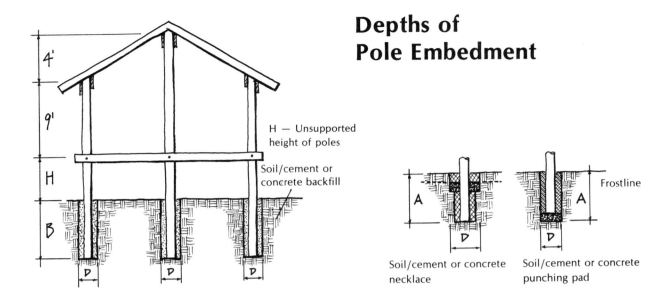

Depths of Pole Embedment

H — Unsupported height of poles

Soil/cement or concrete backfill

Frostline

Soil/cement or concrete necklace

Soil/cement or concrete punching pad

Depth of Pole Embedment—Fairly Flat Site

"H"	Pole Spacing	Good Soil Embedment Depth A	B	"D"	Tip Size	Average Soil Embedment Depth A	B	"D"	Tip Size	Below Average Soil Embedment Depth A	B	"D"	Tip Size
1½′	8′	5.0′	4.0′	18″	6″	6.5′	5.0′	24″	6″	*	6.0′	36″	6″
to	10′	5.5′	4.0′	21″	7″	7.0′	5.0′	30″	7″	*	6.5′	42″	7″
3′	12′	6.0′	4.5′	24″	7″	7.5′	5.5′	36″	7″	*	7.0′	48″	7″
3′	8′	6.0′	4.0′	18″	7″	7.5′	5.5′	24″	7″	*	7.0′	36″	7″
to	10′	6.0′	4.5′	21″	8″	8.0′	6.0′	30″	8″	*	7.5′	42″	8″
8′	12′	6.5′	5.0′	24″	8″	*	6.0′	36″	8″	*	8.0′	48″	8″

* Embedment depth required is greater than 8 feet, and considered excessively expensive.

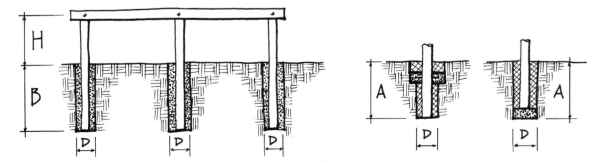

See table top of next page.

Depth of Pole Embedment—Platform Building—Fairly Flat Site

"H"	Pole Spacing	Good Soil Embedment Depth		"D"	Tip Size	Average Soil Embedment Depth		"D"	Tip Size	Below Average Soil Embedment Depth		"D"	Tip Size
		A	B			A	B			A	B		
1½	8'	4.0'	4.0'	18"	5"	5.5'	4.0'	24"	5"	7.0'	5.0'	36"	5"
to	10'	4.5'	4.0'	21"	5"	6.0'	4.0'	30"	5"	8.0'	5.5'	42"	5"
3'	12'	5.0'	4.0'	24"	5"	6.5'	4.5'	36"	5"	*	5.5'	48"	5"
3'	8'	5.0'	4.0'	18"	6"	6.5'	4.5'	24"	6"	*	6.0'	36"	6"
to	10'	5.5'	4.0'	21"	7"	7.0'	5.0'	30"	7"	*	6.5'	42"	7"
8'	12'	6.0'	4.5'	24"	7"	7.5'	5.5'	36"	7"	*	7.0'	48"	7"

* Embedment depth required is greater than 8 feet, and considered excessively expensive.

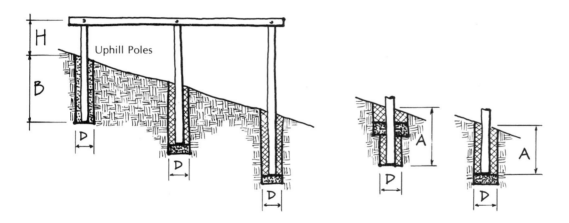

Depth of Pole Embedment—Platform Building—Sloping Site—Uphill Poles

"H"	Pole Spacing	Good Soil Embedment Depth		"D"	Tip Size	Average Soil Embedment Depth		"D"	Tip Size	Below Average Soil Embedment Depth		"D"	Tip Size
		A	B			A	B			A	B		
1½	6'	5.5'	4.0'	18"	6"	7.5'	5.0'	18"	6"	*	7.0'	24"	6"
to	8'	6.5'	4.5'	18"	7"	*	6.0'	24"	7"	*	8.0'	36"	7"
3'	10'	7.0'	5.0'	21"	7"	*	6.5'	30"	7"	*	*	*	*
	12'	7.5'	5.5'	24"	8"	*	7.0'	36"	8"	*	*	*	*
3'	6'	7.0'	5.0'	18"	8"	*	6.5'	18"	8"	*	8.0'	24"	8"
to	8'	7.5'	5.5'	18"	9"	*	7.0'	24"	9"	*	*	*	*
8'	10'	*	6.0'	21"	10"†	*	7.5'	30"	10"†	*	*	*	*
	12'	*	6.5'	24"	10"†	*	*	*	*	*	*	*	*

* Embedment depth required is greater than 8 feet, and considered excessively expensive.
† These tip diameters may be decreased one inch, providing embedment is increased by one-half foot.

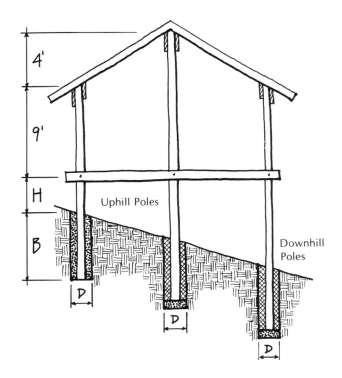

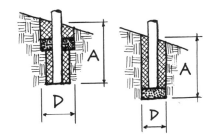

H—Unsupported height of uphill pole

A—Embedment depth, using backfill of tamped earth, sand, gravel, or crushed rock

B—Embedment depth, using backfill of concrete or soil/cement

D—Bearing diameter

Depth of Pole Embedment—Sloping Site—Downhill Poles

Soil Strength	Slope of Grade		
	Up to 1:3	Up to 1:2	Up to 1:1
Below Average	4.5'	6.0'	–
Average	4.0'	5.0'	7.0'
Good	4.0'	4.0'	6.0'

Depth of Pole Embedment—Sloping Site—Uphill Poles

"H"	Pole Spacing	Good Soil				Average Soil				Below Average Soil			
		Embedment Depth		"D"	Tip Size	Embedment Depth		"D"	Tip Size	Embedment Depth		"D"	Tip Size
		A	B			A	B			A	B		
1½'	6'	7.0'	5.0'	18"	8"	*	6.5'	18"	8"	*	*	*	*
to	8'	7.5'	5.5'	18"	9"	*	7.0'	24"	9"	*	*	*	*
3'	10'	*	6.0'	21"	9"	*	8.0'	30"	9"	*	*	*	*
	12'	*	6.5'	24"	10"†	*	*	*	*	*	*	*	*
3'	6'	7.5'	5.5'	18"	8"	*	7.0'	18"	8"	*	*	*	*
to	8'	8.0'	6.0'	18"	9"	*	8.0'	24"	9"	*	*	*	*
8'	10'	*	7.0'	21"	10"†	*	*	*	*	*	*	*	*
	12'	*	7.0'	24"	11"†	*	*	*	*	*	*	*	*

* Embedment depth required is greater than 8 feet, and considered excessively expensive.

† These tip diameters may be decreased by one inch providing embedment is increased by one-half foot.

Maximum Depth of Frost Penetration (Inches)

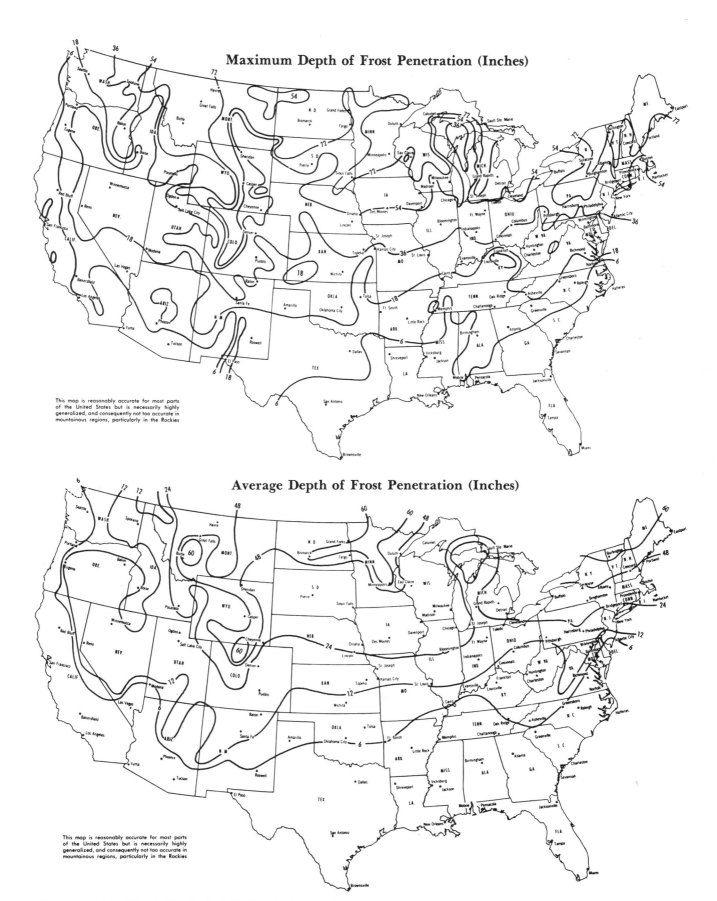

This map is reasonably accurate for most parts of the United States but is necessarily highly generalized, and consequently not too accurate in mountainous regions, particularly in the Rockies

Average Depth of Frost Penetration (Inches)

This map is reasonably accurate for most parts of the United States but is necessarily highly generalized, and consequently not too accurate in mountainous regions, particularly in the Rockies

Source: Strock and Koral, *Handbook of Air Condtioning, Heating and Ventilating*, 2nd Edition. Industrial Press Inc. New York, N.Y.

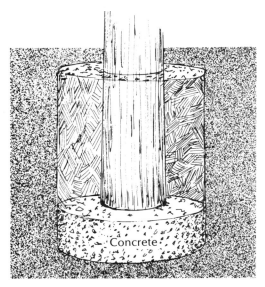

Footings for the poles. Heavy flat stone or poured concrete punch pad should be provided for each of the pole holes before the poles are placed, unless soil is very solid. Thickness of footing should be at least one-half the diameter of the pole.

Jane and Paul mix the concrete for the pole footings, then pour it into the holes.

Setting and Aligning the Poles

After your pole house is completed, filled with people and pianos, and piled high with snow on the roof, each pole may be carrying as much as six tons of weight. Even in the best soil, some settling is unavoidable. The trick is to avoid excessive or uneven settling, which could cause extensive structural problems.

In very good soil (hard dry sand and clay, gravel or coarse sand, or hard rock), a single-story house with moderate pole spacing may be built with the pole butts resting directly on the bottom of the holes. For lesser soils or heavier loads, pour a concrete footing pad at least half as thick as the pole butt diameter. In either case, be sure that the pole or footing rests on undisturbed soil. Filling in a too-deep hole creates a soft layer of earth that will cause the pole to settle unduly. Don't bother with a form for the concrete; just use the hole walls as the form.

When the concrete has cured, it's time to wrestle the poles into place. Invite several strong friends over for the day. Provide them with work gloves and beer. Some ingenuity may be required to erect the poles in their holes. A block and tackle, hitched to an overhanging tree or to a temporary tripod, may make things much easier. Some pole-builders have used a truck to pivot the poles up into position. For maximum embedment strength, it is important to minimize damage to the dirt walls of the hole. To prevent the pole from gouging out soft earth as it is tilted into position, use skids of smooth lumber to guide it.

Use the straightest poles at the corners, butt end down. The straightest side of the pole should face out unless the walls will stand inside the poles, in which case the inner facing sides should

Patrick drills a hole in the butt-end of the pole, which will fit over a galvanized steel J-bolt embedded in the footing. This method prevents the butt from slipping out of position. Be sure to flood the bored hole thoroughly with pentachlorophenol.

be the straightest. If a pole must be rotated, wrap rope around it and use a wooden lever bar to avoid scarring the pole.

When the pole is vertical, pack a few inches of soil around the butt; just enough to keep the pole from shifting. Do not embed the pole yet. Use a four-foot carpenter's level placed on a straight-edge to plumb the poles as accurately as possible; then nail temporary braces to the poles and to stakes in the ground, to keep the poles lined up until framing is completed. Locate this bracing outside the guidelines where it won't interfere with the work.

The last pole is raised into place.

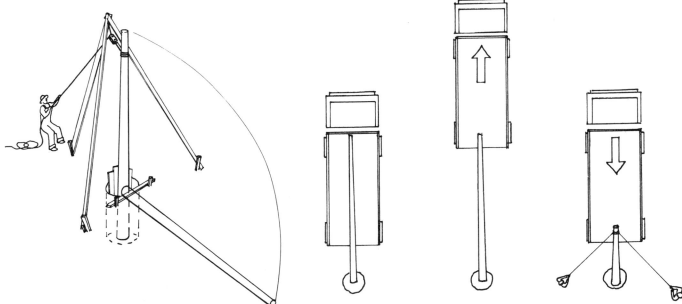

Erecting the poles using a block and tackle. The pulley may be attached to an overhanging tree, if convenient. For maximum embedment strength, use wooden skids as shown to prevent damage to the walls of the hole.

Erecting the poles using a truck. With the tip of the pole resting on the tailgate, the truck slowly backs up, angling the pole upward. Use skids to prevent damage to the edge of the hole, and guide ropes to control the pole as it goes up.

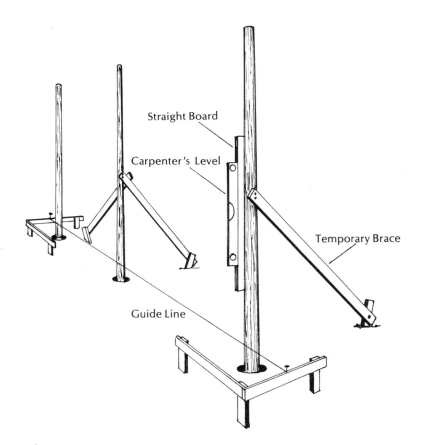

Straight Board

Carpenter's Level

Temporary Brace

Guide Line

Aligning the poles. If sheathing will be installed outside the poles, the outside faces of the poles must be vertical. If the walls will stand inside the poles, however, the inside faces should be vertical.

Attaching the Girders

Carpenters live by three key words: square, plumb, and level. The careful builder is continually checking these three requirements, knowing that they'll make subsequent work a lot easier. Layout of the pole locations helps establish a square building. Alignment of the poles establishes a plumb structure. These first two can be refined somewhat as the building is constructed. But an accurate level *must* be established; since this is difficult to change later, it should be done now with great care.

Determine a level line on all the poles, eighteen to twenty-four inches above the highest point of ground. The most accurate method is to use a *clear plastic tube* filled with water. Hold the ends upright against two poles; water in the two ends of the tube will be exactly level. Or a *carpenter's level* placed on a long straightedge can be used. A *line level* is the least accurate. To minimize error, pull the string taut and place the line level in the center of the string. Reverse it to check for error.

Eighteen inches clearance between the ground and the floor girder is minimum; twenty-four inches would make it easier for you to crawl under the house when it is completed. Once this level reference line is established, measure up carefully to locate the position of the upper girders.

The outside roof girders at the eaves are attached first. Mark the location of the girders' lower edges, then nail the temporary cleat (of 2×4 or 2×6 and approximately thirty-six inches long) to the pole to support each girder until it is bolted or spiked in place.

Girders should be cut so that their ends will

Wendell installs temporary bracing as Patrick and Kevin hold the pole in a plumb position.

butt together at the poles. The girders at the corners of the building should extend beyond the poles to support the last rafter.

Rest the girders on the temporary cleats and spike or bolt them to the poles. Now remove the temporary cleats. Pre-boring the nail holes in the girders will minimize the danger of splitting the wood, yet will not decrease the holding power. Use a 5/32-inch drill bit for 40d nails.

Where heavy snow or wind may be expected, or where load-bearing floors are supported by the poles, bolts rather than nails are advised to attach girders to the poles. Lag screws with washers also may be used. Eaves girders on the *inside* of the poles are not installed until after the rafters are in place.

Install the ridge girders next, using the same procedure. Determine the height to the bottom of the ridge girders (as for the eaves girders), and nail cleats of 2 × 4 lumber on each side of the cen-

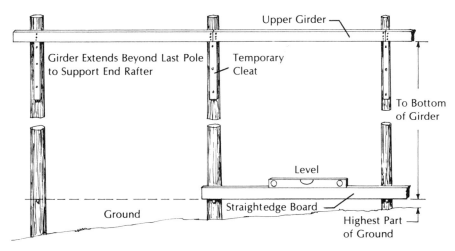

Getting the ground level. Carpenter's level establishes true line for sill.

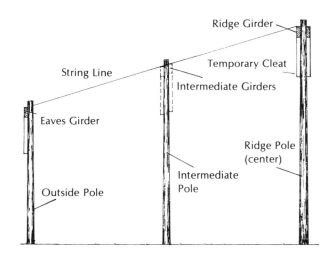

Locating girders on intermediate poles. If the building has intermediate poles, locate ridge girders and eaves girders first. Then stretch a string taut between them, and mark the location of the intermediate girders.

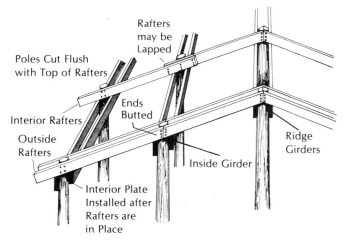

Bolt or spike rafters to the poles, then add rafters every 16 or 24 inches, or as needed to accommodate roof sheathing. Compound rafters may be lapped or butted, as shown.

ter poles. Rest the girders on these cleats and fasten them with spikes, bolts, or lag screws. Stagger the joints in any double set of girders so that there is only one joint at each pole.

When the building is so wide as to require extra inner poles, the position of the roof girders on these intermediate poles can be located by running a string from the ridge girder to the eaves girder. Attach cleats and girders on both sides to correspond to this line.

Rafters

Rafters are placed adjacent to each pole, plus intermediate rafters as required. If plywood is to be used for roof sheathing, space the rafters sixteen or twenty-four inches on center so that the plywood edges butt over a rafter. Extend the lower ends of the rafters over the outside girders at the eaves to provide an overhang—usually about ten to fourteen inches.

Rafters placed on the outside of the end wall poles should be butted to provide a smooth base for exterior siding. Cut the butt ends of the outside rafters to the proper angle (the same angle as the plumb cut for the ridge), so that the rafters may be nailed to the poles. Intermediate rafters may be lapped if spacer blocks are used and the plywood edges won't butt over the rafter.

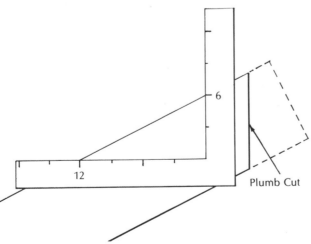

Using a rafter square to obtain the correct angle for the plumb cut of the rafters on a 6/12 roof.

Trim the pole tops after the roof framing is in place.

Ralph hoists the hip rafter into position. A temporary scaffold holds up the roof peak until all four hip rafters are in place.

The angle cut at the upper end of the rafter, called the *plumb cut,* may be determined by the roof pitch, using a rafter square. Or you could simply hold the first rafter in place at the ridge, and use a level or plumb line to mark the plumb cut. When the first rafter is cut correctly, use it as a template to cut all the others to the same angle.

Rafters adjacent to the pole should be nailed to the pole. Anchor other rafters to the girders by means of metal straps or by two-inch scab boards (or ties), fitted between the girders. When rafters are in place, the poles may be cut off flush with the tops of the rafters. Finally, install the inside girders at the eaves. Push the girders up against the rafters, remembering to stagger the joints, and attach them to the poles.

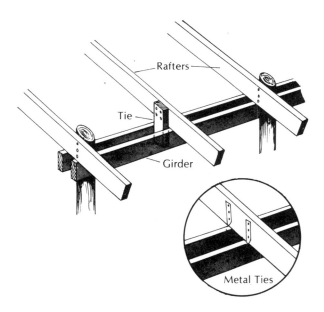

Attaching rafters to girders.

When hip rafters are in place, the rest of the rafters are installed.

Trim the rafters and attach the fascia. A scaffold makes this job easier.

Pole Embedment

After the rafters are in place, complete the embedment of the poles. Proper setting and embedment of the poles is crucial to the strength of the building frame. If poles are embedded to the recommended depth, no additional wind bracing is required in the structure.

The pole embedment carries three kinds of forces:

1. *Downward,* under the weight of structure, snow, furnishings, and occupants.
2. *Upward,* when a hurricane-force wind may cause uplift on the structure.
3. *Sideward,* as moderate or heavy winds push against the building.

In order to resist upward and sideward forces, the embedment backfill must be very firm and compact.

If adequate embedment is not possible, some form of supplementary wind-bracing must be installed. Knee braces or plywood gussets should be installed on the inside of the poles. Nail or bolt two pieces of 2×4 four feet long at each end. When there is a wide center space in the structure an additional knee brace or gusset should be attached to the pole on each side of the center space. Gussets are better than knee bracing, since they provide greater strength at the hinge points, and they are no more difficult to cut and install.

You may backfill the holes with the soil dug from the holes, or with sand, pea gravel, or crushed rock to assure good drainage around the pole. Sand is the cheapest and compacts very well when flooded with water, provided that sur-

rounding soil offers good drainage. When earth is used it must be compacted, a little at a time, by wetting and careful tamping.

Some authorities recommend backfilling with concrete or soil/cement (a 5:1 mixture of sifted earth and cement with water). When concrete is poured around a pole, however, it swells with moisture. After the concrete has cured, the pole shrinks away from the concrete, leaving a gap for water to accumulate. Furthermore, over-use of concrete defeats the inherent economy of pole construction. For these reasons, we do not recommend using concrete or soil/cement to backfill.

Another popular method of backfill uses a "necklace" of concrete around the pole below the frost line. It can be cast after the poles are set but

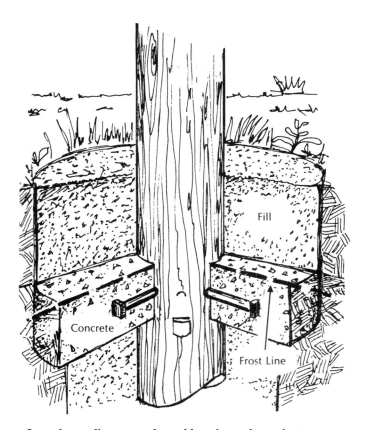

In moderate climates a pole necklace is an alternative to a concrete footing. After the poles are set and partially filled in, cast a 12-inch-thick concrete necklace around the pole. Lag screws assure good connection with pole. Make sure that the necklace lies below the frost line.

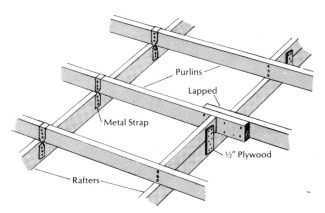

not fully filled in. This necklace should be at least twelve inches thick. A minimum of four one-inch diameter galvanized lag screws around the pole are required to transfer the vertical force to the necklace.

The necklace method is practical only in areas where the frost line does not exceed two feet. It would be difficult to cast such a necklace at a depth of three feet or more.

Two methods of anchoring purlins to rafters. When rafters are spaced farther than twenty-four-inches apart, purlins are needed to support one-inch wood sheathing, metal or other types of roofing. Purlins are laid across the rafters and are either lapped or butted, as shown. Rafters may be spaced up to eight feet with no purlins if two-inch roof decking is used.

Roof Pitch

Roofs range in slope, or *pitch,* from dead flat to nearly vertical. The pitch of a roof is expressed as a fraction which represents the amount of vertical *rise* per foot of horizontal *run.* Thus, a 1/12 roof is very low-pitched, rising only one inch in twelve inches of run; a 6/12 roof is much steeper, rising six inches for every twelve inches of horizontal distance (or six feet in twelve feet, or sixty feet in 120 feet). A flat roof presents formidable waterproofing problems, and is not recommended in cold climates. A steep roof sheds water and snow easily, and the space enclosed is more usable than the cramped attic under a low-pitched roof. But in very cold climates it may be advantageous to retain the blanket of snow on the roof. Asphalt shingles require a pitch of at least 4/12. For roofs with a pitch between 2/12 and 4/12, roll roofing should be used.

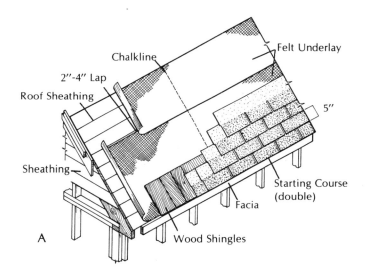

Roof Sheathing and Shingling

There are several alternatives in roof construction:

● Rafters spaced sixteen or twenty-four inches on center, covered with one-inch sheathing or ½-inch plyscore of sheathing grade. The spacing

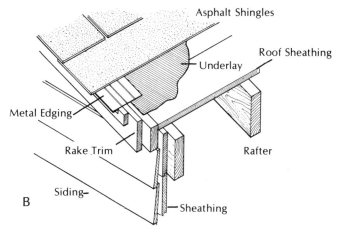

Application of asphalt shingles: A, normal method with strip shingles; B, metal edging at gable end.

also allows sixteen or twenty-four inch rolls of fiberglass insulation to be inserted between the rafters. Stagger the joints in the plywood sheets, and leave a nail's-width gap between sheets to allow for thermal expansion.

● Rafters spaced wider than twenty-four inches, carrying *purlins*. The rafters must be stronger, since they are spaced further apart. Purlins are laid across the rafters and are either lapped or butted. Wood sheathing, metal or other types of roofing are then nailed to the purlins.

● Rafters spaced up to twelve feet apart with three-inch *roof decking* above. This method uses more material, but much less labor. It also presents an attractive underside if no ceiling or insulation is to be added later. Two-inch decking can span up to eight feet. Check with the supplier to determine maximum span of the decking; it varies with the wood species. If only slight insulation is desired, add a plastic vapor barrier, then a layer of one-inch styrofoam sheathing board on top of the decking. This method leaves the underside of the decking exposed to the interior. Longer nails will be needed for the shingles (see page 82).

With the roof sheathing in place, shingling can begin. Asphalt shingles are easy to apply. Read the instructions printed on the package, or ask at the lumberyard. To avoid unwanted variations in color, make sure that all the bundles come from the same batch. Roll out layers of tar paper parallel with the lower edge of the roof, overlapping them until the sheathing is covered. Then use the guidelines on the tar paper to assure that the shingle rows are parallel. Start early in the morning, take a long mid-day break to avoid the heat of the sun, then put in a few more hours in late afternoon. Besides avoiding discomfort, you will avoid damaging the shingles by walking on them when the tar is soft.

Floor Construction

As with the roof, several alternatives are available:

● The floor may simply be compacted earth, as for a barn or toolshed.

● A concrete slab may be poured.

● The floor may be suspended on girders and joists, like the roof.

If these buildings are to be in cold climates, construction should be planned with a view to effective floor insulation.

It is difficult to insulate a dirt or concrete floor. But if the site is level, these floors are the cheapest. The concrete slab should rest on well-compacted gravel and a polyethylene vapor barrier. If heavy vehicles are to drive on the slab, reinforce it with a six-inch mesh of welded wire fabric. The slab should be at least four inches thick.

To construct a suspended floor, first attach the floor girders to the poles with spikes, bolts or lag screws, just as the roof girders were attached. Install temporary cleats, stagger the joints, pre-bore the holes for bolts or spikes before mounting the girders in place.

Next, install the floor joists. These may be hung from metal framing anchors between the girders, or the joists may rest on top of the girders. The latter method allows the joists to cantilever out beyond the girders, and transfers their load to both of the girders. This design increases the load capacity of the floor, but raises the floor several inches, and so the building must be that much

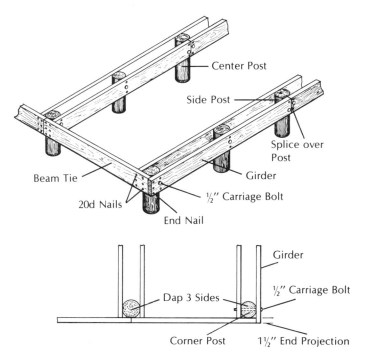

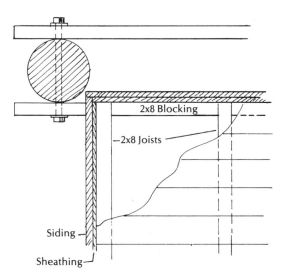

Floor girders may be attached with spikes, bolts, or lag screws.

Attaching floor girders to poles. In this case, walls go inside poles to make it easier to finish the interior walls.

Bill spikes together the doubled 2 x 12 floor girders.

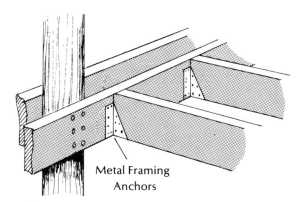

Metal Framing Anchors

Anchored floor framing. These suspended joists will not support as heavy a floor load, because they are carried only by one girder.

After the diagonal joists are in place, the other floor joists are cantilevered over the girders.

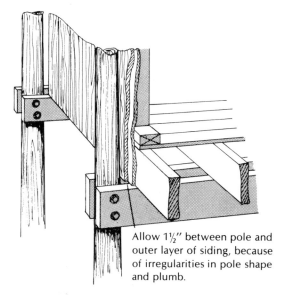

Allow 1½″ between pole and outer layer of siding, because of irregularities in pole shape and plumb.

One method of constructing a suspended floor. Joists rest on top of floor girders, permitting them to cantilever out as much as one-half the span. Joists must be braced with blocking or cross-bridging between them.

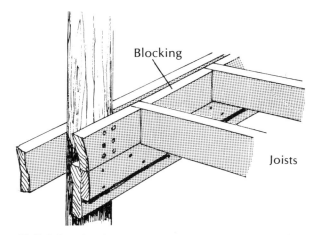

Blocking

Joists

Nailed floor framing. Supporting joist-ends here rest on a floor girder. Blocking keeps them upright.

taller. Furthermore, it is necessary to insert blocking or cross-bridging between the floor joists to keep them standing on edge. If the space between poles exceeds six feet, a 2×4 is placed on each 2×6 for reinforcement.

The use of metal framing anchors avoids the need for cross-bridging and the additional height. But the anchors transmit the load onto only one of the girders. They are one more thing to buy, and are somewhat inelegant. But neither method is better than the other; take your pick.

If plywood is to be used for subfloor, make sure that the joists are spaced sixteen or twenty-four inches on center. Or use tongue and groove plywood, and plywood supports (see section on Fastenings). In either case, use ⅝-inch plywood. If boards are used for subflooring, joist spacing is not crucial—though conventional spacing allows easy use of fiberglass floor insulation later.

The floor may be left as plywood, or may be finished with hardwood flooring, carpet, quarry tile, or vinyl.

Detail of the floor framing, showing a 4 x 4 block cut into an octagon shape sitting atop the short center pole. Diagonal joists are 2 x 12, the rest are 2 x 8; their top edges are flush.

After the floor joists are installed, mark them with a string line and cut the ends off evenly.

Walls

Because the walls carry no roof load in a pole building, they need only be substantial enough to resist strong winds, and may be built in any of several ways.

To enclose a building with a dirt or concrete floor, install *splashboards* at the ground line. Starting about six inches below grade and extending up the wall, spike splashboards to the poles, using pressure-treated lumber. These should be one or two 2×10 or 2×12 planks. On a slope, step the splashboards to match the grade.

The next step is to nail *girts* across the poles above the splashboards to carry the siding. They should be spaced two feet or four feet on center, depending upon local wind conditions and the type of siding to be used. Generally speaking, metal siding will require two-foot centers, while wood can be on four-foot centers. Consult table on page 85 to determine the type of girt to use.

Frame openings for windows and doors using 2×4 or 2×6 vertical studs nailed to the splash board and girts or upper girder. Try to plan the spacing of girts so that they act as headers or sills for the doors and windows. Reinforce the splash board under the door; it will get a lot of wear as a threshold.

Then install siding of vertical boards and battens, plywood or metal siding to the girts and splashboards. Factory-made windows and door frames may be installed in the framed openings, or you may construct them yourself.

Girt construction may be insulated with fiberglass batts cut to size and stapled in place, or with foam insulation applied to the inside surface of the siding. If interior wall finish is to be ap-

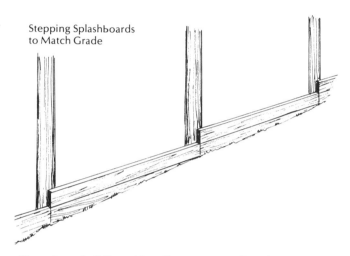

To enclose a building with a dirt or concrete floor, install preservative-treated splashboards at ground line.

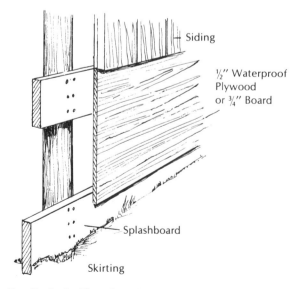

Detail of splashboards and of exterior sheathing method is shown here. Note pressure-treated lumber should be placed below the ground line.

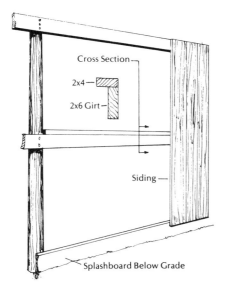

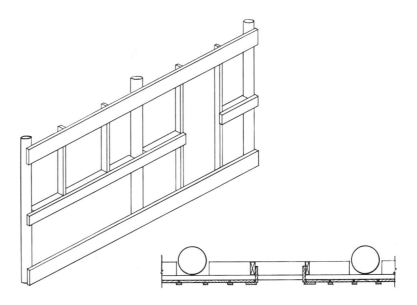

Attaching girts. Illustrated here is the use of girts between the poles to support the sidewall sheathing. Shown in cross-section is the reinforcement of a girt.

Girt construction, framing of doors and windows. Try to plan girt location so that they can act as headers and sills for doors and windows.

Peg and Brigid assemble the wall sections on the floor.

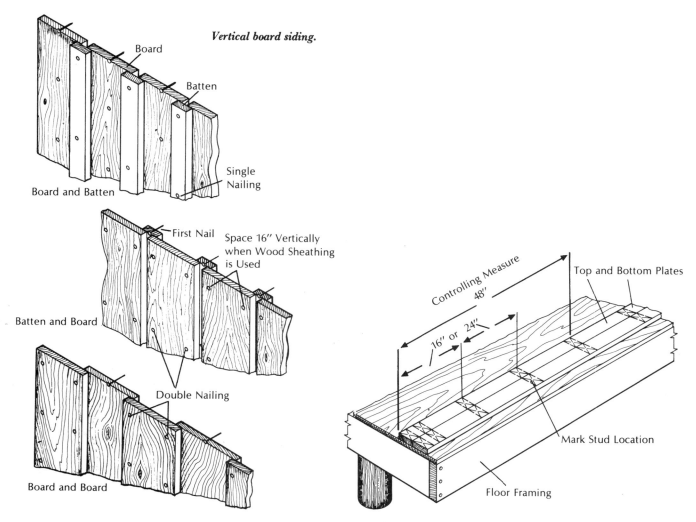

Vertical board siding.

Board

Batten

Board and Batten

Single Nailing

First Nail

Space 16" Vertically when Wood Sheathing is Used

Batten and Board

Double Nailing

Board and Board

Note: Nail for First Board—8d or 9d
Nail for Second Board—12d

Controlling Measure 48"

16" or 24"

Top and Bottom Plates

Mark Stud Location

Floor Framing

Once the platform is completed, standard stud framing may be built upon it.

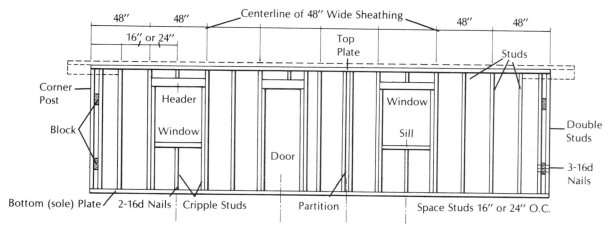

Centerline of 48" Wide Sheathing

48"   48"   48"   48"

16" or 24"

Top Plate

Studs

Corner Post

Header

Window

Block

Window

Sill

Door

Double Studs

3-16d Nails

Bottom (sole) Plate   2-16d Nails   Cripple Studs   Partition   Space Studs 16" or 24" O.C.

Framing layout of typical wall, using conventional stud construction.

The assembled wall sections are tilted up into place.

plied, the wall cavities may be insulated with blown-in cellulose, vermiculite or fiberglass and a vapor barrier.

Girts also may be used to frame walls on a suspended-floor building. Or build stud frame walls, just as you would in conventional construction. The wall sections may be assembled on the platform, then tilted up into place. Frame out doors and windows as you would normally. Because the walls are not load-bearing, no headers are required above door and window openings, and a single plate and shoe will suffice. The studs may be 2×4s spaced twenty-four inches rather than sixteen inches on center, making these walls cheaper in labor and materials than conventional load-bearing stud construction. See illustrations, or consult a book on carpentry for instructions. Stud frame walls are easier to insulate and to apply interior wall finish. They also allow the wall to stand independent of the poles. This is an advantage if the poles are crooked. And from an aesthetic standpoint, you may prefer it. But stud

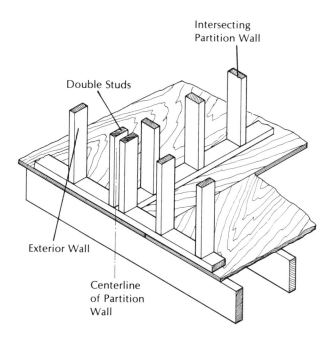

Intersecting
Partition Wall

Double Studs

Exterior Wall

Centerline
of Partition
Wall

Stud wall construction. Use double studs at wall intersections to provide nailing surfaces for edges of interior wallboard.

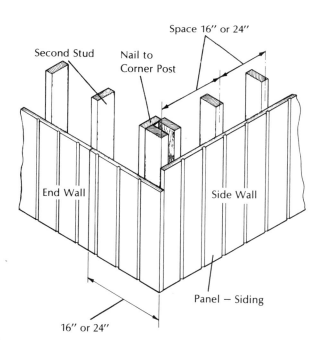

Second Stud

Nail to
Corner Post

Space 16″ or 24″

End Wall

Side Wall

Panel — Siding

16″ or 24″

Exterior side and end wall intersection, using stud wall construction.

wall construction involves more material and labor than the girt system.

Wherever walls meet poles, *shims* may be necessary to fill in gaps due to pole variation. For small gaps, shims may be tapered cedar shingles; larger gaps may require one or more thicknesses of plywood to fill in the crack or straighten the line. You can use a taut string to measure unevenness along a line of poles, or press a straightedge against the pole to spot the gaps. Shims also can be used where a plumb wall meets a non-plumb pole. Extensive shimming can be a tedious job; if appearance or weather-sealing is important, it is best to use a wall system which permits easy and accurate wall construction not dependent on the poles for alignment.

Mike nails the wall section into place.

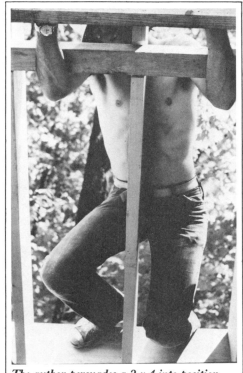

The author persuades a 2 x 4 into position.

Photo by Will Paxson

Laura relaxes on the porch of Camp Cabin 1.

Photo by Will Paxson

Check with the local building department before beginning the wiring.

9

Plumbing and Electricity

These trades are not as difficult as you may think. If you are handy, you may be able to do the plumbing and electrical work yourself with the help of a few books. You will save some money and learn something in the process. But if you are unsure of your work, ask a pro to take a look before hooking up the system. Check with the local building department; some areas require that all electrical work be done by a licensed electrician, others have no code. Even if you decide to leave it to the experts, learn about these systems so you can plan your interior layout for economy and convenience. Consult the Bibliography for some useful references.

Plumbing and electric wiring are generally installed after the building is framed, but before the inside walls have been finished. Plumbers and electricians drill holes in studs, joists, and rafters, fishing their lines through the holes from source to fixtures. It may look sloppy, but it will all be hidden by the wallboard—*if* you plan to install wallboard. Tell your subcontractors if you don't, so that they can be a little neater.

Electric service arrives at the house by over-head or underground wire, and leads to a master circuit-breaker panel controlling all circuits in the building. Major electricity users include furnace, hot-water heater, pump, and oven. Try to locate these items close to the panel box for economy. If you contemplate a windmill in the future, study up on the subject so your present system is compatible with your future plans. Avoid excess use of electricity.

Water arrives at the house through a pipe from a well or the town water mains. If it is well water, the pump may be submerged in the well or located in the house with a holding tank. City water arrives under pressure, and no pump is needed. The supply pipe then branches into two; one for the cold water, the other to enter the hot water heater.

Hot water may be heated by gas, oil, electricity, or the sun. Electricity is usually the most expensive of the four. Solar hot water is now economically competitive with electricity in all parts of the country. Gas is also considerably cheaper than electricity.

Oil-fired hot water heaters are usually cheaper

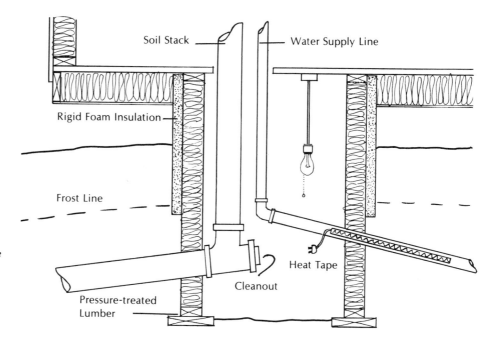

Soil Stack

Water Supply Line

Rigid Foam Insulation

Frost Line

Hotbox: To keep pipes from freezing, you may enclose and insulate them to below the frost line, keeping them warm with the heat from a light bulb. In this drawing, heat tape has been installed for emergency thawing. Use pressure-treated lumber throughout.

Heat Tape

Cleanout

Pressure-treated Lumber

to operate, but aren't commonly used because they require installation of a fuel oil tank. If the house will be heated with oil, furnace and water heater could share a single large tank. Most furnaces offer the option of hot-water heating as a way to utilize waste heat. This is very efficient in winter when the furnace is normally operating. But in summer, it is wasteful to fire up the oil or gas furnace just to heat water. Best solution: hook up the hot water heater in series with the furnace, which acts as a pre-heater. In winter, the furnace heats the water and the water-heater never turns on. Whenever the furnace is cold, the water heater does the work.

To minimize plumbing, group all fixtures together in the house. If possible, back toilets, sinks, and bathtubs to a single "wet wall," containing all the plumbing. This wall will have to be somewhat thicker than normal to accommodate the waste lines. In a two-story house, stack the bathrooms.

Two waste pipes are installed: a *soil stack,* which goes straight down into the ground and then underground to the town sewer or a septic tank and leach field; and a *vent stack,* which goes straight up through the roof to vent gases and odors.

Freezing Pipes

The danger of pipes freezing, a familiar concern to homeowners in all but the warmest climates, is of special importance in a pole building. Because these pipes must pass through an uninsulated crawl space, they are exposed to the cold for several feet before dropping below the frost line. If your water supply line freezes in midwinter when the ground is frozen solid, you may be without water until the spring thaw.

There are several ways to protect these pipes against freezing. In mild climates it may be sufficient to group the water supply pipe, soil stack, and all other piping below the house to drop to grade at one point only, well back from the house perimeter. Insulate this bundle of pipes well, with a material impervious to moisture and rotting, such as rigid foam. Urethane Molding, Inc. of Laconia, NH manufactures *Insuljac®,* insulated pipe jackets designed to protect water lines from freezing. The urethane insulation is protected by a casing of tough PVC plastic, and can be slipped over any kind of metal or plastic piping.

A regularly used soil stack will receive some warmth from waste decomposition in the septic tank, and should not freeze. And because well water is usually at least 45° F., even in midwinter, the flowing water in an active water line will not freeze. When the flow ceases for a period (during the night or when no one is home), the water in the lines can gradually cool to below freezing, no matter how much insulation there is. In cold climates, further protection is necessary.

Three alternatives are available: keep the water flowing at all times during cold spells, heat the pipes, or drain them when not in use.

The first method is an unacceptable waste of water, may deplete some wells, and may dilute or overload some septic systems, causing a freeze-up in the soil line.

To heat the pipes, wrap them with *heat tape* (a strip of tape containing an electrically heated wire) inside the pipe's insulation. Choose a heat tape which can be thermostatically controlled, so that it doesn't burn needlessly during warmer months. Or build a *hotbox* to enclose and insulate the pipes, and heat them with a light bulb. In a well-insulated hotbox, the slight heat of the light bulb should be sufficient to prevent freezing. Leave a peekhole so you can check that the bulb is still burning. Or enlarge the hotbox into a mini-basement, and place the furnace or hot water heater down there to keep the pipes warm. The hotbox also could be left open to the house's warmth if it is well-insulated.

If the house is unoccupied for periods in the winter, design the entire plumbing system to allow drain-down. It is wasteful to heat a building just to keep the pipes from freezing.

Some owners manage to avoid the problems of plumbing and electricity entirely. They heat and cook with wood, use a composting toilet, and haul water from a well. And lighting with an oil lamp is more efficient than burning oil in a power plant to generate electricity.

Photo by Ehrlich-Rominger Architects

10

Heating and Cooling

Whether or not you plan to heat or cool your building mechanically, be sure to design it to take advantage of the sun and wind to be warm and sheltered in winter, shaded and breezy in summer. Natural ventilation, aided by a house fan, can take the place of air conditioning in many climates. And solar energy can provide some or all of the house's heating needs.

Passive solar heating systems heat a house by simple methods, without need of elaborate and expensive collectors or gadgets. Solar heat is collected directly in the space, and stored in massive floors or walls, tempering and stretching the day's heat into the night. But such massive elements are incompatible with the house-on-stilts nature of pole building.

One alternative is to use water to store the heat. Vertical tubes or racks of steel drums are filled with water and placed behind south-facing windows. Water has a great capacity to retain heat, and has the further advantage that it heats evenly, distributing its warmth throughout the vessel by natural convection. For this reason, a *water wall* has certain advantages over a concrete Trombé solar wall. Plans for a passive solar pole cottage are shown on page 167. Or consult the Bibliography for books about solar energy.

Wood heat is the easiest fuel alternative for a small cabin or a vacation home, especially if you have a woodlot of your own. Approximately one cord per acre per year may be harvested without depleting the forest; thus a small house may require seven to ten acres of forest for self-sufficiency. Modern wood-burning stoves extract maximum heat value from each log. Fireplaces are much more wasteful, unless they are heatilator-type air circulating fireplaces with glass doors and an outside air combustion inlet. Wood-burning furnaces or boilers are also available, as are dual-fuel systems using wood and oil or gas.

Central heating systems are of two types: forced air and hot water. Forced air systems use furnaces; hot water systems use boilers. Forced air systems use large metal ducts to carry the air through the house. These can be somewhat cumbersome; placed overhead, they are clunky and visible. Placed under the floor, they must run be-

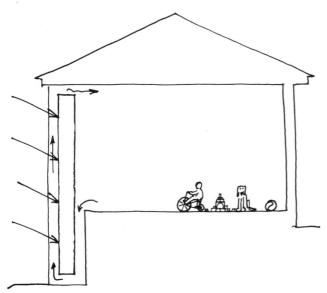

Michel-Trombé wall combines solar collection and massive heat storage.

The water wall, *like Trombé wall, absorbs heat during the day and releases it during the night.*

low the insulation to avoid the joists. Unless heavily insulated, the ducts will lose much heat to the cold outdoors. But air systems have an advantage: the same ducts can be used for central air conditioning in the summer.

If you don't plan to install central air conditioning, choose a hot-water heating system. Finned pipes carry hot water in baseboards around the perimeter of the house, taking up much less space than the bulky ducts. If a portion of the house is to be seldom used, install a two-loop heating system so the heat may be shut off in

that portion. An automatic setback thermostat will lower the temperature at night or during the day when the house is unoccupied, and quickly pay for itself in saved fuel.

In warm or moderate climates, a heat pump is much more efficient than a standard air-conditioner, and also may be used to heat the house during a mild winter. Some manufacturers now offer water-source heat pumps. These units achieve great efficiency by using 60° F. well or pond water as a cooling source, rather than 95° F. air. In winter, they can use 50° F. well water as a heating source, rather than 20° F. outside air.

You'll save even more if you confine the air conditioning to only a portion of the house, like the bedroom, to provide a cool retreat on the hottest days. The rest of the house can be opened up to capture the breeze.

Insulation and Weatherproofing

If you plan to heat or air-condition your pole house, take care to insulate it adequately. Insulation is a better investment than a savings account, and skimping is false economy.

The appropriate insulation strategy varies with climate, building type and use. Consult the Bibliography for more information on conserving energy.

Pole buildings present a few specific insulation problems. In a suspended-floor pole building, the underside of the floor is exposed to the elements. Fill the joist spaces with fiberglass insulation (vapor barrier side *up*, toward the house) and seal the undersides of the joists with plastic, plyscore, or insulating sheathing. Or place rigid insulation boards and a vapor barrier *on top* of the subfloor and cover with the finish floor.

A skirt board around the crawl space will greatly reduce heat loss through the floor. Cover the earth under the house with polyethylene sheet held down with rocks to inhibit the rise of moisture into the floor. Allow a few vents in the

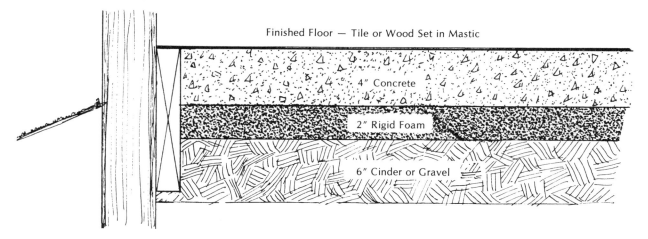

Floor built on grade requires vapor seal below concrete.

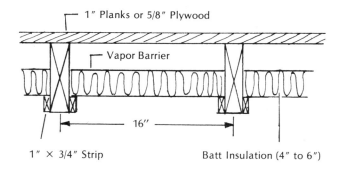

Open floor is insulated from below with batts hung between joists.

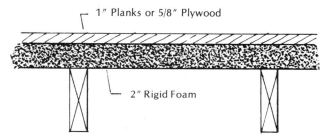

Alternate method places rigid foam atop joists and below flooring.

skirt board to dissipate any moisture which does accumulate.

Examine all joints in the house for possible leaks of cold air. Pay particular attention to places where poles penetrate the skin of the house. Stuff fiberglass or other insulation around large cracks, and caulk the smaller ones. Don't forget holes around plumbing inlets and kitchen and dryer vents. In cold climates, install storm windows or double glazing. For even greater savings, add insulating shutters or drapes. Caulk and weatherstrip around all doors and windows, and caulk all the construction joints (where floor meets wall, wall meets roof, and so on). In a cold climate, include a vestibule in your house design.

Because a pole house does not rely on the walls for wind-bracing, the plywood sheathing may be replaced by insulated sheathing-board for additional insulative value.

You may wish to construct a small half-cellar of masonry to house the furnace, water heater and pump, and to protect the plumbing lines

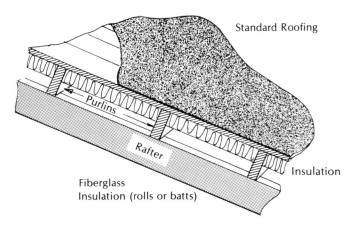

Insulating the roof. Batt insulation is set between roof purlins or rafters, below sheathing.

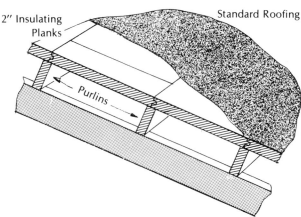

Alternate method dispenses with batts, uses insulating plank in place of standard roof sheathing.

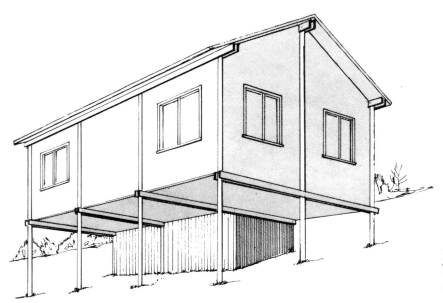

Furnace, water heater, pump and plumbing connections may be enclosed in a half-basement utility room below the floor, if desired.

from freezing. However, such a solution is inelegant, and involves expensive masonry work of the kind that pole building is supposed to avoid. Nowadays furnaces can be clean, silent, odorless, and small. It's not necessary to build a basement to hide one.

This, then, is the general summary of pole construction, and the methods are the same whether you're building a chicken coop or a house. Garden Way Associates' industrial designer, who illustrated the previous pages, has prepared plans of example pole buildings, which follow. Other plans may be obtained from some of the sources listed in the Bibliography. Now that you know the basics of pole building, you may prefer to design your own. Use the tables below to size the lumber for your design. Look at the illustrations throughout this book for ideas and details, then improvise. Draw measured plans and details; it helps speed the building process, and heads off big mistakes.

Tables

The following tables should allow you to size the girders, joists, and rafters of your pole building. The figures given are based on the use of Douglas fir #2, a common and very strong species of wood. If you cannot use Douglas fir or larch, decrease the spans somewhat to allow a margin of safety. Choose better grades of lumber for greater strength.

Table 1: Floor Joists — Maximum Span
(clear distance between supports)

Joist size	At 16" o.c.	At 24" o.c.
2×6	8' 10"	7' 9"
2×8	11' 8"	10' 2"
2×10	14' 11"	13' 0"
2×12	18' 1"	15' 10"

For Douglas Fir/Larch #2, repetitive-member use. $F_b = 1450$ psi, $E = 1.2$
40 psf live load; 19% moisture content.

Table 2: Rafters — Maximum Span — Light Snow Load
(20 psf live load)
Note: span is measured horizontally, even on sloped roofs.

Rafter size	At 16" o.c.	At 24" o.c.
2×6	12' 9"	10' 9"
2×8	17' 0"	14' 6"
2×10	21' 5"	18' 6"
2×12	26' 0"	22' 0"

Douglas Fir/Larch #2, repetitive members, 19% moisture. $F_b = 1450$, $E = 1.2$

Table 3: Rafters — Maximum Span — Moderate Snow Load
(30 psf live load)

Rafter size	At 16" o.c.	At 24" o.c.
2×6	11' 0"	9' 6"
2×8	14' 10"	12' 8"
2×10	18' 11"	16' 0"
2×12	23' 0"	19' 6"

Douglas Fir/Larch #2, repetitive members, 19% moisture, $F_b = 1450$, $E = 1.2$

Table 4: Rafters — Maximum Span — Heavy Snow Load (40 psf)

Rafter size	At 16" o.c.	At 24" o.c.
2×6	10' 2"	8' 7"
2×8	13' 5"	11' 3"
2×10	17' 1"	14' 6"
2×12	20' 9"	17' 6"

Douglas Fir/Larch, repetitive members, 19% moisture, $F_b = 1450$, $E = 1.2$
Note: in some areas of very heavy snowfall, these maximum spans should be
reduced.

Table 5: Girders Carrying Joists or Rafters

Case A: Joists or rafters are carried by a pair of girders.

Pole spacing	Girder size
8 feet	use 2×6's
10 feet	use 2×8's
12 feet	use 2×10's
14 feet	use 2×14's or 3×10's
16 feet	use 3×12's

Case B: Joists or rafters are carried by a single girder;
Intermediate pair of girders, carrying two spans of joists;
Joists or rafters are cantilevered over a pair of girders as far as one-half the pole spacing.

Pole spacing	*Girder size*
8 feet	use 2×10's
10 feet	use 2×12's
12 feet	use 2×14's or 3×12's
14 feet	use 3×14's
16 feet	use 4×14's

(Douglas Fir/Larch, as above. 40 psf live load, 20 psf dead load.)

Table 6: Wall Girts — Maximum Span to Resist Heavy Winds

		Design Wind Pressure			
Girt type	*Girt Spacing*	*15 psf*	*20 psf*	*25 psf*	*30 psf*
2×6	2' o.c.	8'	7'	6'	5'6"
	4' o.c.	5'6"	5'	4'6"	4'
2×6 + 2×4	2' o.c.	13'	11'	10'	9'
	4' o.c.	9'	8'	7'	6'6"
2×6 + 2×6	2' o.c.	17'6"	15'	13'6"	12'6"
	4' o.c.	12'6"	11'	9'6"	9'

Douglas Fir/Larch #2, 19% moisture, repetitive use.

II.

Examples of Pole Building

In the illustrations of pole structures that follow, a great variety is evident. Some are simple one-room cottages designed and built by rank amateurs. Others are elaborate and expensive architect-designed houses. A few are not houses at all.

These buildings and sketches are presented as a source of ideas. If you plan to construct a pole house, look through these illustrations and borrow a few ideas. Remember that there are many correct ways to build a house.

Pawleys Island house

In 1962 the Forest Service constructed this pole dwelling in Pawleys Island, South Carolina, as an experiment in the feasibility of pole building. It is a good example of simple and straightforward construction methods.

Left: *Detail showing dapping of the corner pole.* Below: *Floor joists are framed between the paired girders.* Bottom: *Carpenters install the end rafters. Walls are framed with 2 x 4 studs.*

Steen house

The Hawaiian home of Gordon R. Steen, reminiscent of native Polynesian house design, provides for efficient natural ventilation through ceiling ducts. The pressure-treated poles (here using a water-borne salt preservative) are unpainted and reach from their footings on the steep slope to the high roof beams.

Construction from start to finish took about eight weeks. The outside and interior poles were set first, roof beams were then attached, the deck system cantilevered from the poles, floors bolted to the poles and the walls attached last.

Architects for the home were Black, Pagliuso, Kikuchi and O'Dowd of Honolulu.

Opposite: *Each room opens onto an outdoor deck. Access to the house is by stairway from above.* Left: *The airy, open inside roof area also allows updraft ventilation. Note that the heavy beams are attached with structural metal anchors to each other and to the interior poles.* Below: *Tropical forest lies just outside this corner bedroom's deck. The textured redwood walls hang from inside faces of exterior poles, as does the decking.*

Hull house

This vacation home for a family of five overlooks Hingham Bay near Boston. The extremely narrow and steeply sloping lot led architect Richard Owen Abbott, Boston, Massachusetts, to employ pole construction and a highly unusual interior design.

The Hull house is eighty-one feet long but only twelve feet wide. A deck runs along the waterfront side, which itself is 75 percent glass. The back of the house is shingled but without windows. Louvers provide ventilation.

The back of the home rests on a concrete pier bearing wall, while the front is supported by eleven thirty-foot poles which have been pressure-treated with Koppers' pentachlorophenol in liquefied butane.

Opposite: *End view shows the steepness of the lot and the narrow dimension of the house.* Left: *Triangular deck at house's center is seen from the steep slope below. Note that the treated poles are set in concrete.*

Left: *Interior of the long, narrow house is divided into eight bays of about ten by twelve feet each. Only the bathroom is partitioned. Walkway along the waterfront side expands into a deck, right foreground.* Below: *The site plan.*

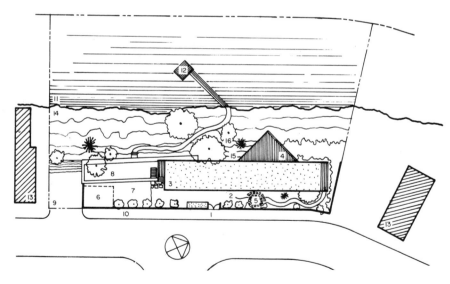

1. Wrought Iron Site Entrance Gate
2. Main House Entry
3. New House
4. Deck
5. Breakfast Outdoor Dining Terrace
6. Canvas Covered Outdoor Studio
7. Grass Court

8. Lower Level Terrace
9. Off-street Parking for Two Cars
10. 6' High Fence
11. Mean High Water Line
12. Boat Landing and Float
13. Existing Structures
14. Property Lines

15. Grass Slope Under House
16. New Landscaping at Front Consists of Lavell Hawthorne and European White Birch (Clump, Weeping, and Single) and Japanese Black Pine.
   At Rear Pin Oak and Japanese Black Pine.

Richardson house   Fresh out of architecture school, Bill Richardson built this pole house in Whitesburg, Kentucky, as a demonstration of economical construction methods appropriate to the hilly country of Appalachia.

Above: *Architect Richardson shows a visitor where the windows will be placed.* Right: *Side view of the house during construction.*

Kent house

The Wendel Kent house is located on LaCosta Island, Florida. Accessible only by boat, the house was designed by Edward J. Seibert so that it could be built without heavy construction equipment. Square in plan, this simple cottage is topped with a cupola to admit light and cool breezes.

Rain water is collected from the metal roof and stored in a cistern for domestic use.

View of the interior, showing roof framing. In winter the wall panels may be closed.

Photos by Larry Vickers

Vickers house Larry Vickers built this small pole house in the woods of north Florida in 1971 for peanuts, using salvaged lumber and used poles bought from the electric company for $17 each, delivered. It was the first thing he ever built.

Above: *Because the poles carry the weight of the roof, great freedom is possible in framing the walls.* Right: *The front porch.*

Westbrook house Designed by architect Richard Owen Abbott, this flat-roofed house in Westbrook, Connecticut, stands supported by twenty poles on a ten-foot grid. Windows framed right into the poles dramatize the structure, with lightweight wall panels hung between.

Top: *Interior view showing sunken living room, clerestory windows, and attached wall panels.* Right: *Windows are glazed directly into the poles — a very tricky process.* Above: *Cantilevered balcony.*

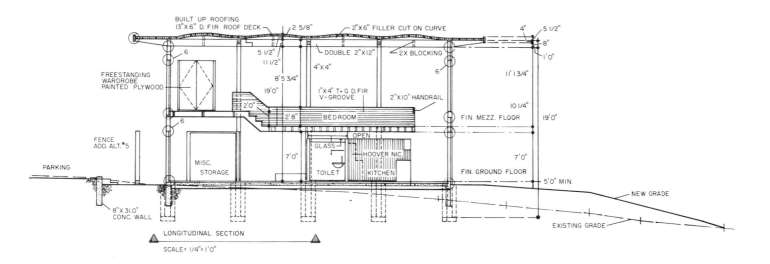

Detail drawings showing typical external timber construction.

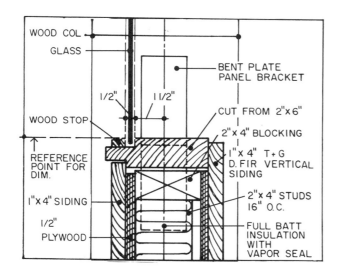

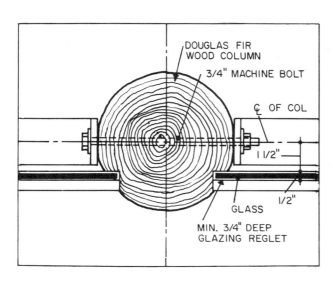

Lebov house

This house employs post and beam construction, a cousin of pole building. Square posts are embedded in the earth, carrying beams which support the roof and walls. George Lebov designed and built this beautiful house himself in North Branford, Connecticut. It was his first attempt at anything larger than a bookshelf. He has recently added a porch deck off the back.

Above: *The living room. Exterior walls contain polyurethane insulation sandwiched between layers of vertical siding.* Top Left: *Detail at corner of ceiling. Roof uses tongue and groove decking beneath a layer of polyurethane insulation.* Bottom Left: *A massive stone hearth in the center of the house contains the fireplace and chimneys. According to Lebov, "When you build with poles, you can afford to spend your money on luxuries like this."*

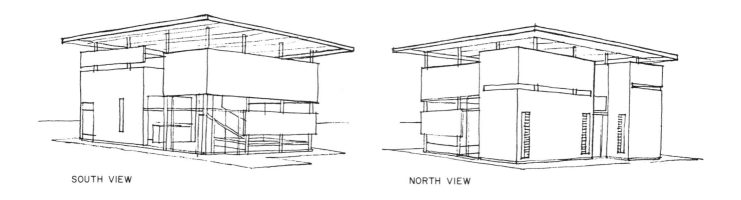

SOUTH VIEW   NORTH VIEW

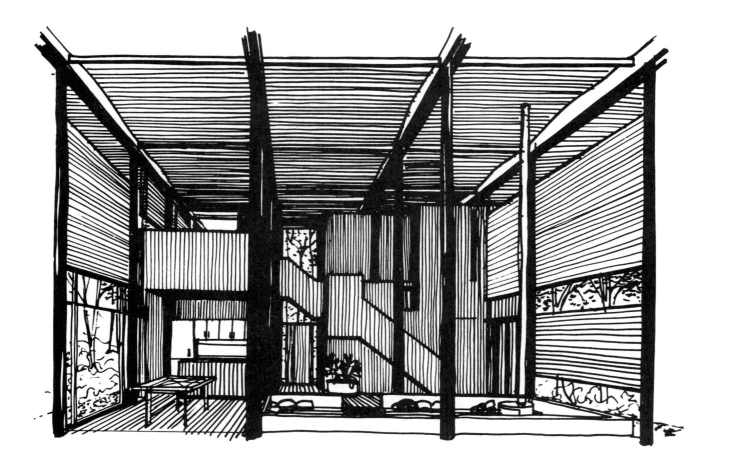

Design for a pole house

This Corbusian scheme by Richard Owen Abbott was never built. Poles dominate the interior like tall trees, with glass and light wall panels filling in between.

Surfside house Built in 1963 by the Forest Service, the Surfside, South Carolina, pole house uses prefabricated roof trusses instead of a ridge girder and ridge poles. This eliminates interior columns and yields a fine house inside and out.

Above: *Pole house in Surfside, South Carolina, under construction. The floor girders have been installed.* **Right:** *Floor joists frame between the girders.*

Left: *In this design, prefabricated roof trusses eliminate the center row of poles.* Bottom Left: *Don't insulate or apply interior wall covering until the inspector has had a chance to look at the wiring.* Below: *Siding is textured plywood.*

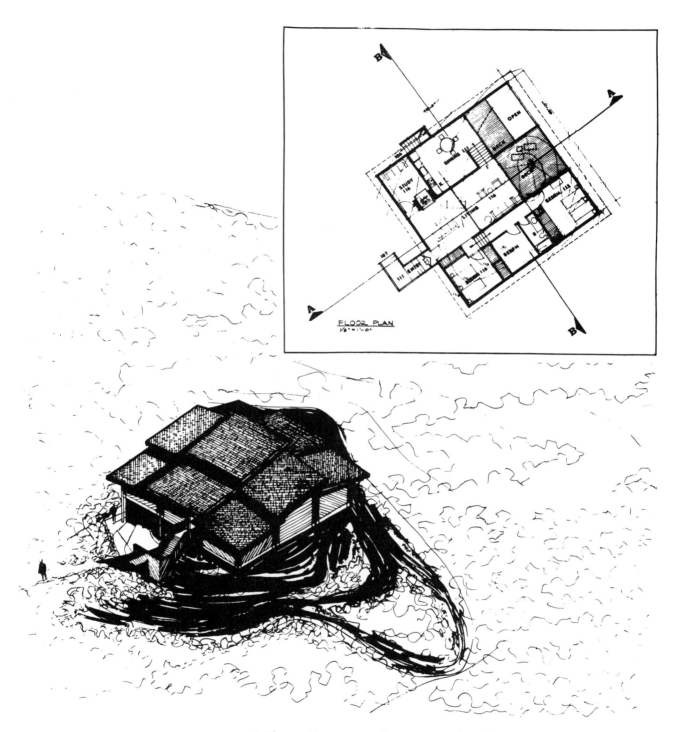

FLOOR PLAN

Nine Square house

Another pole house idea from Richard Owen Abbott, this one based on a nine-square grid, each square with its own roof. Clerestory windows admit light and air at the breaks between the roof segments.

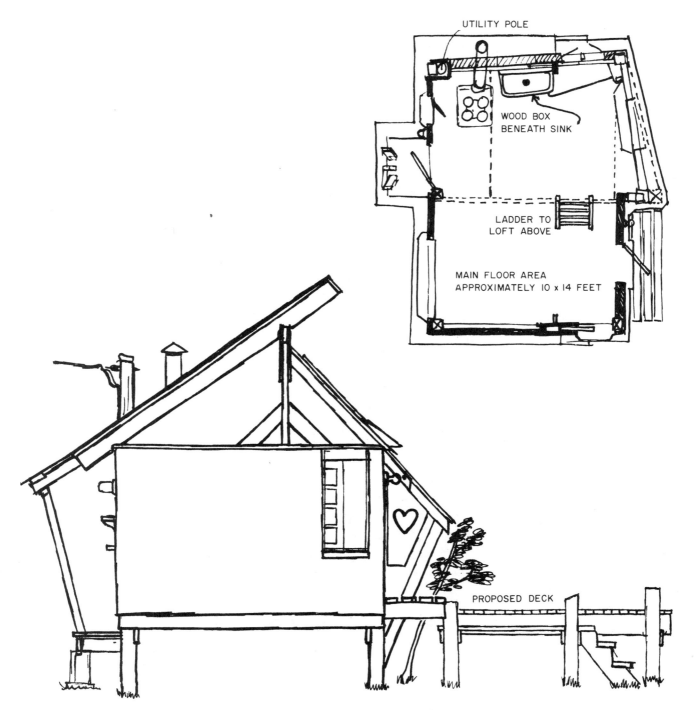

UTILITY POLE

WOOD BOX
BENEATH SINK

LADDER TO
LOFT ABOVE

MAIN FLOOR AREA
APPROXIMATELY 10 x 14 FEET

PROPOSED DECK

Craddock house Kathy Craddock's house in the Florida woods was designed by Larry Vickers. The walls and roof are canted whimsically, providing just enough room for a sleeping loft above the living room/kitchen.

Photo by Louis Reens

Ritz house Only a few poles are vertical in this large and complex house in Greenwich, Connecticut, designed by John Johansen. Because it was impossible to draw the house accurately enough for precision in construction, each pole was hoisted into place and hand-notched in the field. The living spaces were carved out of solid rock. By the time they were placed, the poles cost $1000 each. Trapezoidal shapes of glass are fitted between the poles to enclose the house. And all the poles come together in the center, at the hearth.

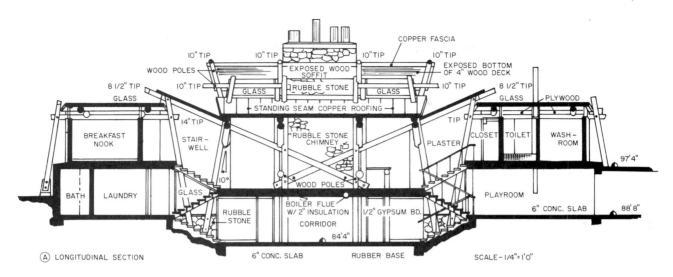

Ⓐ LONGITUDINAL SECTION

Above: *Longitudinal section.* **Left:** *All the poles come together at the fireplace in the center of the house.*

Photos by G. Wade Swicord

MacDonald house

This house employs a deceptively simple design: a square of poles with a large hip roof, which reaches out to cover a wrap-around porch deck. The roof is broken at the peak to light the hall and stairs. Designed by Edward J. Seibert, the MacDonald house is located on Siesta Key, Florida.

Interior view of MacDonald house, showing entry and stairs.

Betsy Ross Nursery School

Don Baerman fashioned this playground out of poles and tires. The result is somewhat reminiscent of the waterfront, with a strong hint of Japanese. Don acknowledges a reference to the Isé Shrine.

Pennsylvania house

The farmland of Bucks County, Pennsylvania, is the location of this International Style residence by Richard Owen Abbott. Three separate wings containing living, sleeping, and utility areas diverge from the center. Most of the poles are exterior to the house, supporting the flat roofs above. Materials are Douglas fir, fieldstone and glass.

Above: *Raised ceiling over the living and dining areas allows clerestory windows above the walls, enhancing light and space inside.*
Right: *Three separate wings contain living, sleeping and utility areas. The poles supporting the flat roofs stand outside the building's walls.*

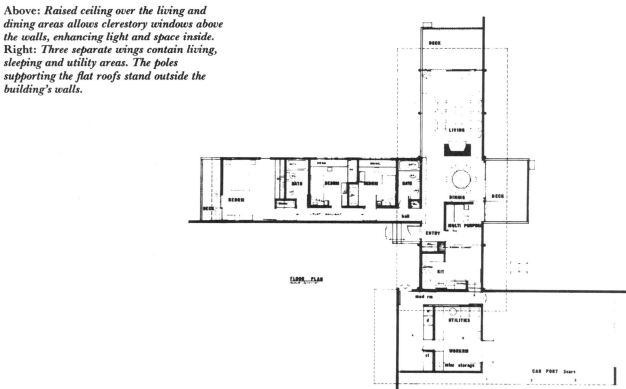

Left: *Detail of the overhanging eaves.* Right: *The roof is sheathed with three-inch decking.*

Korean Church

This capacious Korean Church in Hamden, Connecticut, was designed by Kevin Roche. Paired poles rise inside the sanctuary, dividing nave from aisles. Bamboo screens filter the sun at the glazed gable ends. Three-inch roof decking allows the rafters to be widely spaced.

California house

This version of pole construction makes use of square posts, allowing easier joinery. Ehrlich-Rominger Architects used diagonal wood siding to emphasize the articulation of the house into cubic masses. The design capitalizes on the slight slope by offering three living levels. The middle level is the main floor, reached by a bridge from the parking area.

Left: *This version of pole construction uses square posts for easier joinery.* Below: *Snow on the flat roof gives added insulation.*

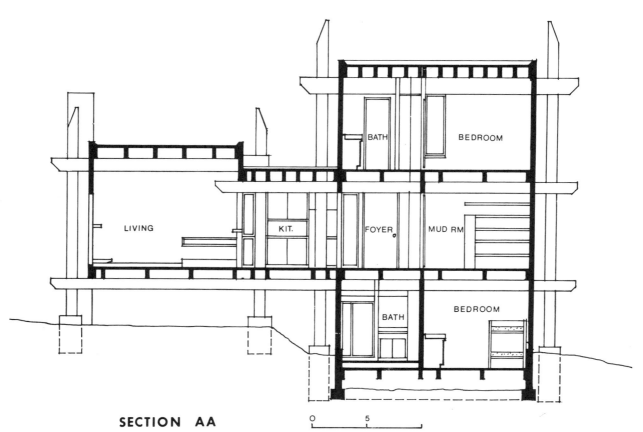

SECTION AA

0   5

UPPER LEVEL

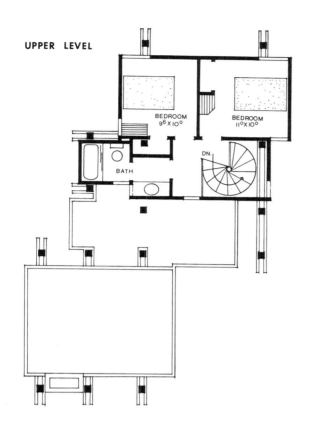

BEDROOM
9⁶ X 10⁰

BEDROOM
11⁰ X 10⁰

DN.

BATH

MAIN LEVEL

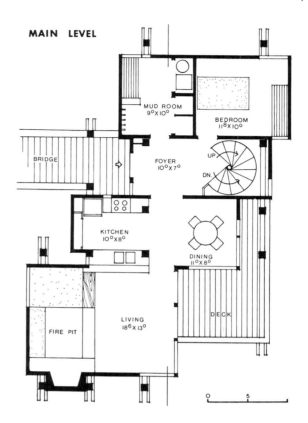

MUD ROOM
9⁰ X 10⁰

BRIDGE

FOYER
10⁰ X 7⁰

UP

DN.

BEDROOM
11⁸ X 10⁰

KITCHEN
10⁰ X 8⁰

DINING
11⁰ X 8⁰

FIRE PIT

LIVING
18⁶ X 13⁰

DECK

0   5

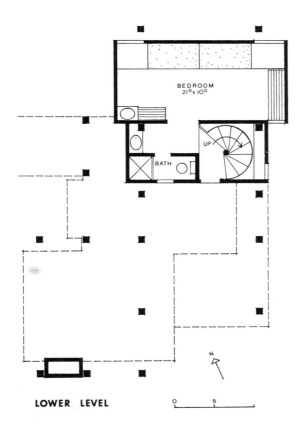

LOWER LEVEL

BEDROOM
21⁰ x 10⁰

BATH

UP

0   5

Above: Lower level floor plan, California house.
Right: The site plan.

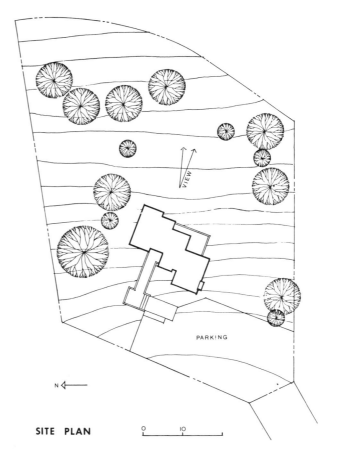

SITE PLAN

VIEW

PARKING

N

0   10

Hexagon house

Richard Owen Abbott designed this hexagonal house as a weekend retreat near Great Peconic Bay on Long Island. Eighteen poles support the roof and main living floor, which is high off the ground, giving a treehouse effect. A small hexagonal core contains the stairs and utility room at the ground level, and a pleasant skylight at the roof.

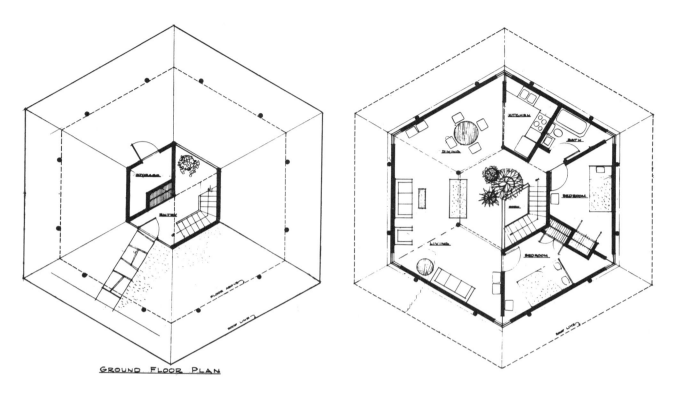

GROUND FLOOR PLAN

Above: *Entrance to the cottage is from below, through the hexagonal stair core.* **Below:** *A south-facing skylight in the roof fills the interior with light.*

WEST ELEVATION
¼" = 1'-0"

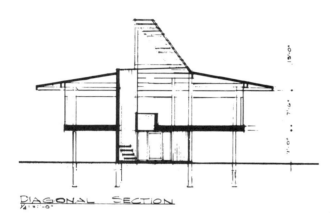

DIAGONAL SECTION
¼" = 1'-0"

CROSS SECTION
¼" = 1'-0"

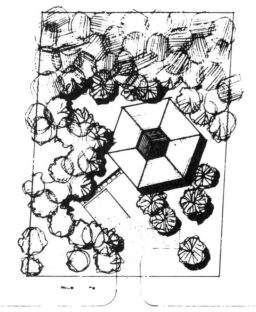

PINE WOOD ROAD

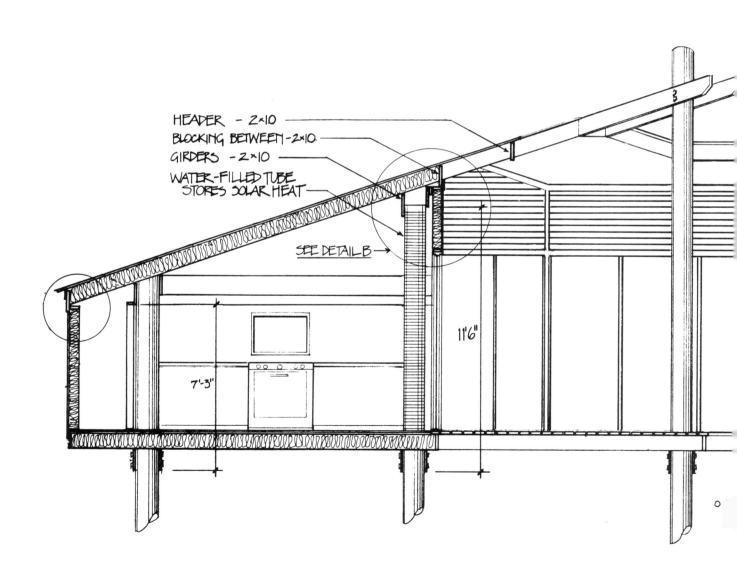

HEADER – 2×10
BLOCKING BETWEEN – 2×10
GIRDERS – 2×10
WATER-FILLED TUBE STORES SOLAR HEAT

SEE DETAIL B →

11'6"

7'-3"

III.

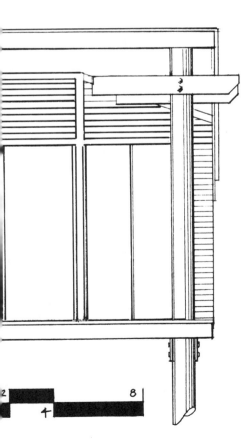

Pole Building Plans

Finished Small Barn. Shed extension to the basic barn can be added later to the main structure, which provides for storage in the roof area.

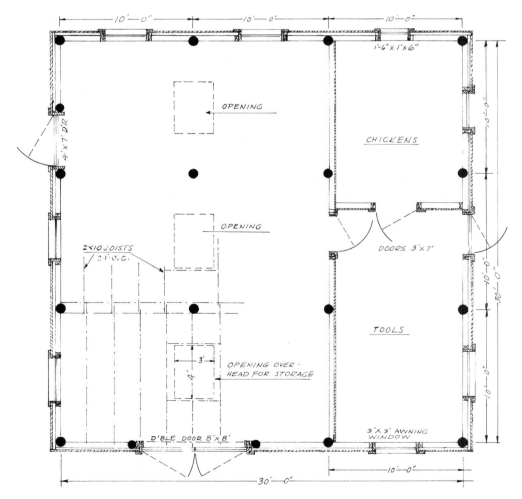

Floor Plan of the Small Barn.
Interior arrangements of the
Small Barn may be modified to
accommodate a variety of uses.
Window and small door
locations are easily altered. But
in locating larger doors,
provision should be made to
locate the wall posts so they will
support the door frame, as seen
at the far left. Other posts are
10 feet apart.

The use of interior posts in
the main barn would permit a
limited amount of storage area
in the roof peak, as with the
Garage (Plan II). This would
be lost if roof trusses are used
in order to provide open floor
area.

If the small barn is built on a
concrete slab — see discussion of
the Garage — and will be used
for the housing of animals,
water supply and drainage
provisions should be planned
and installed in advance.

Small Barn

Here in part is what Ed Robinson of the famous "Have-More" Plan wrote in 1945 about building a small barn: "Once you decide you're going to have some livestock on your place in the country, then it's obvious that you'll need a barn to house it.

"If you're primarily interested in the production of your family's food, you'll want a barn that is small, efficient, inexpensive and designed so simply that you can build it yourself if you so desire. Also, it would be a good idea to construct a barn that could be added to, or easily adapted to some other use.

"If you operate this barn at capacity it will produce more milk, eggs, chicken, lamb, squab, veal, turkey and rabbit than a family can use.

"Many country places already have a structure that can be made into an efficient barn. If you're in doubt as to whether or not it's better to remodel or rebuild, ask a local carpenter for an estimate both ways. If you're going to do the work yourself, pay him for his advice.

"Now, if you are figuring that you might build yourself, let me add a word of encouragement. When we moved to the country and I undertook to build my barn, I actually didn't know the first thing about how to proceed. I had had a course in manual training in grammar school and learned to saw a board and hammer a nail.

"However, I learned that there is nothing complicated about building a small barn or chicken house. If a person has just a little manual dexterity, for instance the ability to drive a car, then he should be able to build a barn with plans."

The 900 square-foot 30×30 barn shown here will provide for the needs of all but the most ambitious homesteader. Unlike the Robinson barn it is a pole construction. Though a section of the interior is labeled, individual demands and desires will vary, so no attempt has been made to plan it completely. The main section could be built first and the lean-to added later.

All the information needed to erect this building is contained in the earlier text. It is important to locate the building so that drainage is away from the foundation in every direction. The floor should have eight inches of gravel under the tamped earth floor. An improvement would be a six-inch concrete floor poured over the gravel.

The large door end of the building requires a somewhat different framing to bridge over the door. And since there is no pole in the center, a beam made of three lengths of 2×8s spiked together is added to support the ridge.

The doors are of the typical barn type made from vertical tongue and groove boards fastened together with battens, with at least one diagonal batten to prevent sagging. The windows are stock sizes available at lumber dealers. Establish the windows' rough opening sizes before nailing on girts, using the windows' vertical dimensions to locate the girts below the plate. Further explanation of this step will be found in the Garage-Toolshed plans, page 137.

Metal roofing can be substituted for the double coverage asphalt shown in these plans. If so, plywood roof sheathing can be omitted, although this is not recommended in cold climates, because of the insulation value and added strength provided by the plywood.

The siding used on the small barn can be board and batten or any of the various textured plywood sidings available for exterior use.

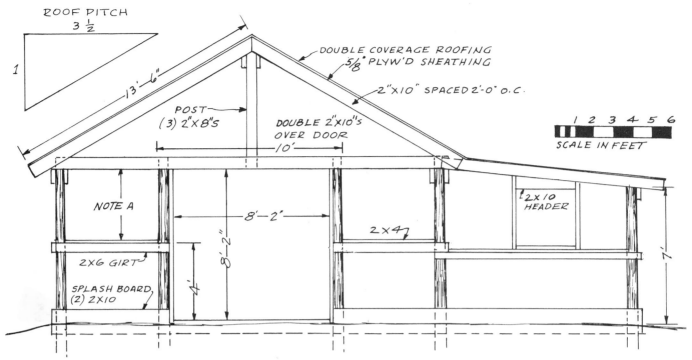

ROOF PITCH
3 ½

1

13'-6"

DOUBLE COVERAGE ROOFING
5/8" PLYW'D SHEATHING

2"X10" SPACED 2'-0" O.C.

POST
(3) 2"X8"S

DOUBLE 2"X10"S
OVER DOOR

10'

1 2 3 4 5 6
SCALE IN FEET

NOTE A

8'-2"

8'-2"

2X10
HEADER

2X4

4'

2X6 GIRT

SPLASH BOARD
(2) 2X10

7'

*Cutaway view of small barn. This section drawing views the main barn from its center.
The windows and batten door are on the far, outside wall. Note that because of the
centered large door at left, a roof beam replaces the full pole there. If a clear floor area is
needed in the main barn, roof trusses would be made to eliminate the two interior poles
shown in the floor plan.*

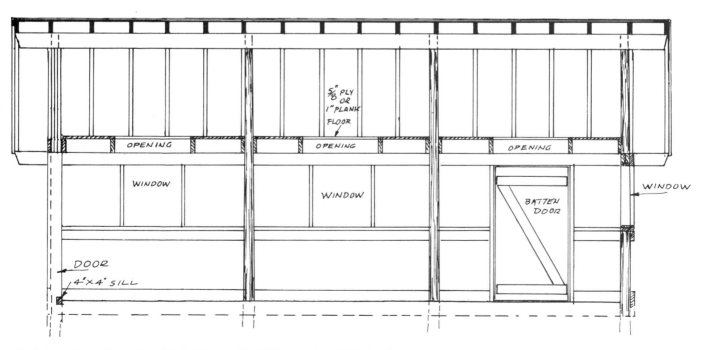

5/8" PLY
OR
1" PLANK
FLOOR

OPENING   OPENING   OPENING

WINDOW   WINDOW   BATTEN
DOOR   WINDOW

DOOR
4"X4" SILL

*End view of small barn. As with the Storage Shed (Plan on page 141) the siding
is on the outside of the poles. Therefore, the poles are aligned so the outside faces are
vertical.*

Multi-Purpose Barn

This 28×40 barn is relatively easy to build (just follow the steps in these diagrams) and can be put to many purposes.

The twelve poles are set twelve feet apart. Buy poles long enough to meet your needs, remembering that for a building of this type, a roof rise of about one foot for every four feet distance is about right.

Study these diagrams, even if you plan to build one of the other structures. Many of the basic principles of pole construction are shown here.

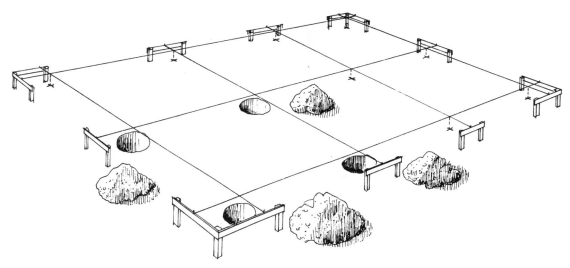

Construct batter boards at the corners, square up the guideline strings, then dig the holes. The strings may be removed for easier digging, then replaced to check hole location accuracy /

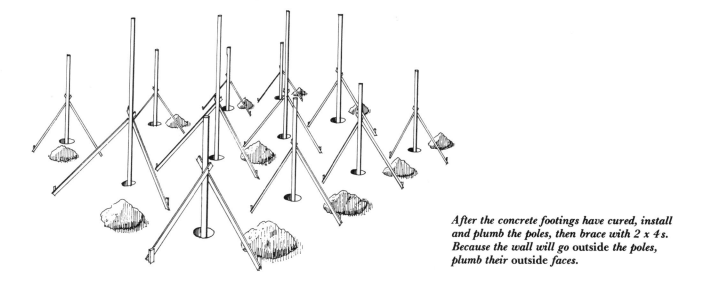

After the concrete footings have cured, install and plumb the poles, then brace with 2 x 4 s. Because the wall will go outside the poles, plumb their outside faces.

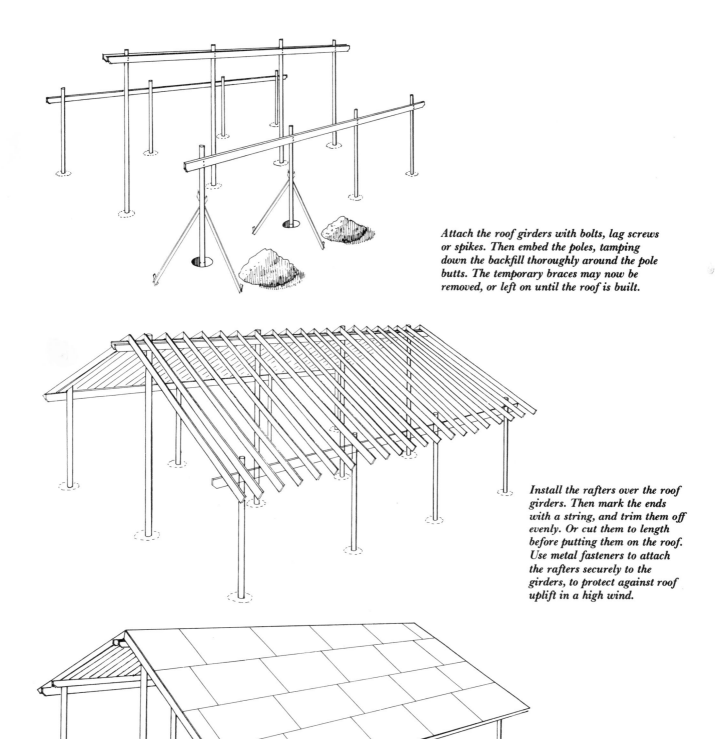

Attach the roof girders with bolts, lag screws or spikes. Then embed the poles, tamping down the backfill thoroughly around the pole butts. The temporary braces may now be removed, or left on until the roof is built.

Install the rafters over the roof girders. Then mark the ends with a string, and trim them off evenly. Or cut them to length before putting them on the roof. Use metal fasteners to attach the rafters securely to the girders, to protect against roof uplift in a high wind.

Nail plyscore sheathing to the rafters. Stagger the seams for greater strenth, and space the sheets 1/16" apart to allow for a little expansion of the wood. The inner roof girders may now be added.

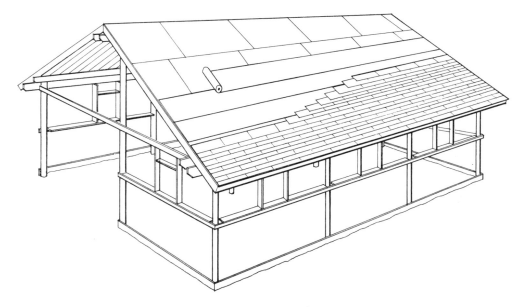

Cover the sheathing with tar paper roofing felt. Take care to roll it out exactly parallel to the roof lines, and staple it down. Use the guidelines on the tar paper to lay out the shingles. Install treated wood splashboards and wall girts to the poles. Frame window openings as desired.

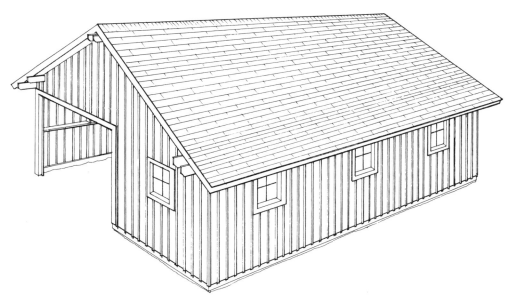

Sheath the walls with vertical board and batten siding. Add windows and doors, and the barn is complete.

Garage with tool shed located at rear. Siding is textured plywood or tongue and groove boards.

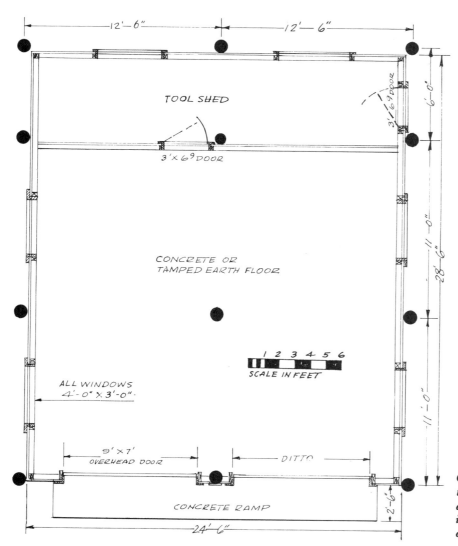

TOOL SHED

3'x6'9 DOOR

3'x6'9 DOOR

CONCRETE OR
TAMPED EARTH FLOOR

1 2 3 4 5 6
SCALE IN FEET

ALL WINDOWS
4'-0" X 3'-0".

12'-6" 12'-6"

6'-0"

11'-0"

28'-6"

11'-0"

2'-6"

9'x7'
OVERHEAD DOOR   DITTO

CONCRETE RAMP

24'-6"

Garage floor plan. Builder may decide to include a hard-surfaced floor, as discussed on page 139. Note that siding is placed inside the poles, except for the center pole between the doors.

Double Garage and Toolshed

A choice of layouts and of roof line is possible in the construction of this building simply by moving the toolshed from the rear to either side, and by switching the location of the poles to match. In this case the distance between the poles from front to back would be eleven feet and from side to side 12½ feet.

This choice will be determined by how best the building fits on your lot, its relation to driveway and house. Note also that in the alternate version rain will drain to the sides of the building. Where the roof slopes toward the doors, a rain gutter would be indicated. In this plan the building is 28½ feet long and twenty-five feet wide.

Farm and country residents may wish to modify the dimensions of this building to accommodate trucks, tractors and other vehicles which require more vertical and lateral clearance than the specified 9×7-foot door openings, which are standard garage door dimensions. Larger overhead garage doors are available from building suppliers, though usually only on special order.

Simple modifications of these plans can be worked out to "stretch" the building both vertically and horizontally in proportions which will not materially alter the one-to-four pitch of the roof. A close calculation should be made in planning any such modifications, however, to determine the increased length needed for poles, planks, boards and sheathing to keep the needs consistent with standard lumber lengths. Bear in mind also that a lesser roof pitch might cause leakage problems in snow country.

Prior to the start of construction of the building, additional plans should be made if there will

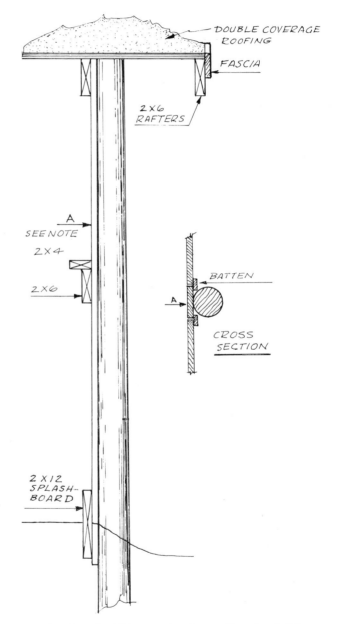

Facing the poles. When erecting the outside poles, nail to them vertically on the inside faces, boards about the same width as the pole diameter. These will help in truing the poles vertically and also will provide the proper clearance between poles, splashboards and girts for the siding.

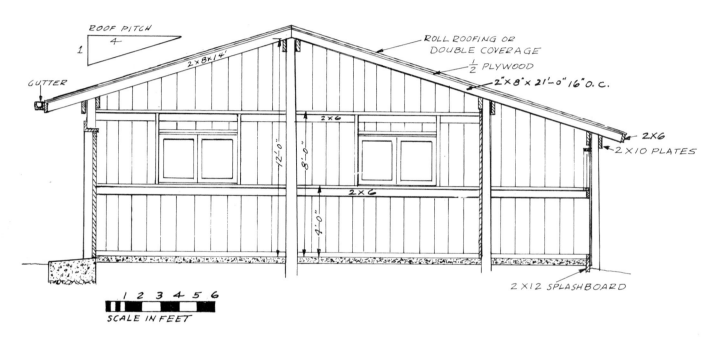

ROOF PITCH
1 / 4

GUTTER

2"x8"x14'

ROLL ROOFING OR
DOUBLE COVERAGE
½ PLYWOOD
2"x8"x21'-0" 16"O.C.

2x6

12'-0"
8'-0"
4'-0"

2x6
2x10 PLATES

2x6

2x12 SPLASHBOARD

1 2 3 4 5 6
SCALE IN FEET

Garage cross-section. This roof is designed to carry a snow load of forty pounds per square foot.

be a need for heat in the toolshed part or the whole structure.

Except in very severe climate conditions a limited heat supply in the toolshed area may be sufficient for most needs, if that room is to contain also a workbench area. Simple insulation of the toolshed walls and roof then is indicated, as well as provision for a small space heater with roof chimney located at the blind end of the shed.

In most cases electricity for lights and power tools will be important. If the building is located near the home the wiring can be brought in by underground conduit and connected (on a new circuit) to the home's central circuit box. Make a determination ahead if there is a possibility that 220-volt service will be needed in the garage for electric heating or other heavy appliances. Otherwise the service wiring should be chosen to carry the maximum anticipated use load in the building.

It is unlikely that a water supply will be required in the garage, particularly if the building is adjacent to the home and a house sillcock is located within fifty feet. Drainage of the garage

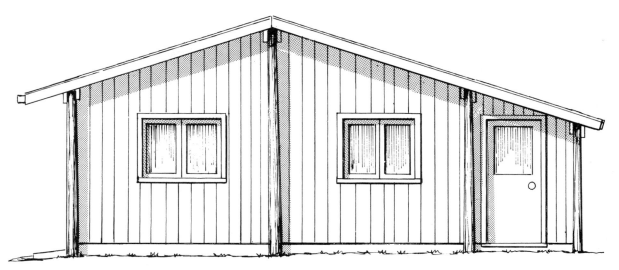

Side view of garage. The tool shed, located at the back in this plan, has its own access door.

Alternate arrangement of garage locates the tool shed to the right or left of the garage doors instead of in the back.

floor area may prove extremely important, however, and provisions should be made if a concrete floor is poured.

Though requiring considerable care in grading, a slab that slopes gently to drain in its center will be the best plan because it keeps water dripping from the garaged vehicles away from the building's exterior wood. Standard iron drain tiles with grill covers are available from most building supply firms.

Concrete floors are prone to cracking in areas where the winters are severe, if subsoil drainage is not good and the gravel pad is not adequate. For this reason, and that it may be cheaper in some areas, a heavy blacktop floor may be a better choice, although it involves installation by a professional paving firm. A packed earth floor may be perfectly satisfactory, however, in climates where rain and snow are not excessive.

A concrete or asphalt garage floor could be added later if the earth floor proves a problem. It will be more difficult to do it once the building is completed, however, and the earth cover would have to be removed first from its gravel base.

Storage shed. This simple seven-pole building could double as housing for small animals or poultry.

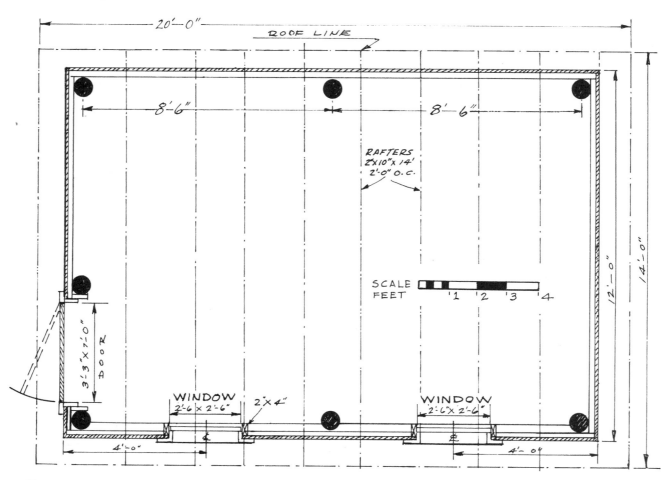

Floor plan of storage shed. Door may be widened merely by relocating center pole at door edge.

Storage Shed

This 12×18-foot shed is designed to provide additional family storage space, as well as providing practical experience in basic pole construction. No attempt has been made to detail the design for a specific need, but it could be adapted or fitted out for housing animals or poultry. Or the shed might be used as a workshop larger than allowed in the Garage-Toolshed plans on page 137.

The poles need not be larger than seven inches at the base for this small building, but all other directions and suggestions in the preceding text should be followed. The best roofing for this type of building considering the shallow slope is "double-coverage" roll roofing. Roughly half of each three-foot strip is smooth tar-coated and the balance has a crushed mineral surface. Start at the lower side of the roof with the smooth portion

of a length of the roll. (The coated half will be used to finish at the peak of the roof.) Cement this down with quick-setting asphalt cement, trimming to the roof edges. A full strip is now laid over this and nailed at the top edge in two 8-inch rows with nails twelve inches apart. Trim at edges, leaving ¼ to ⅜ inch overhang. Continue on to the peak of the roof, finishing with the balance of the first strip.

The siding can be any of several textured plywoods, such as Texture 1-11, or tongue-and-groove siding, or the board and batten type. Windows are difficult to build, and it will be easier to buy some from a salvage building material yard or one of the various stock sizes from a lumberyard.

When locating the pole for the hinged side of the storage shed's door, allow a liberal distance to accommodate the door and frame. As noted earlier, the taper of poles often varies, and it is better to build with shims to the required doorframe width than to find the pole is too close.

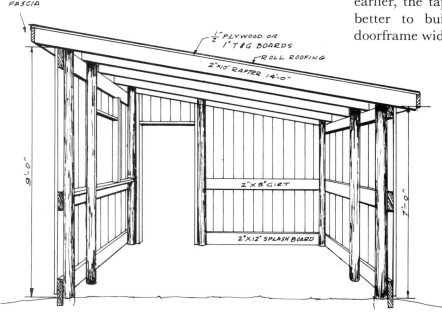

Storage shed, cutaway view. Since siding is applied to the shed pole exteriors, the poles are aligned to keep their outside faces vertical.

Vacation Cottage. High and low sections of the building may be reversed, depending on its orientation to light. On this gentle slope poles rather than a keywall are used on the uphill side as shown on page 28.

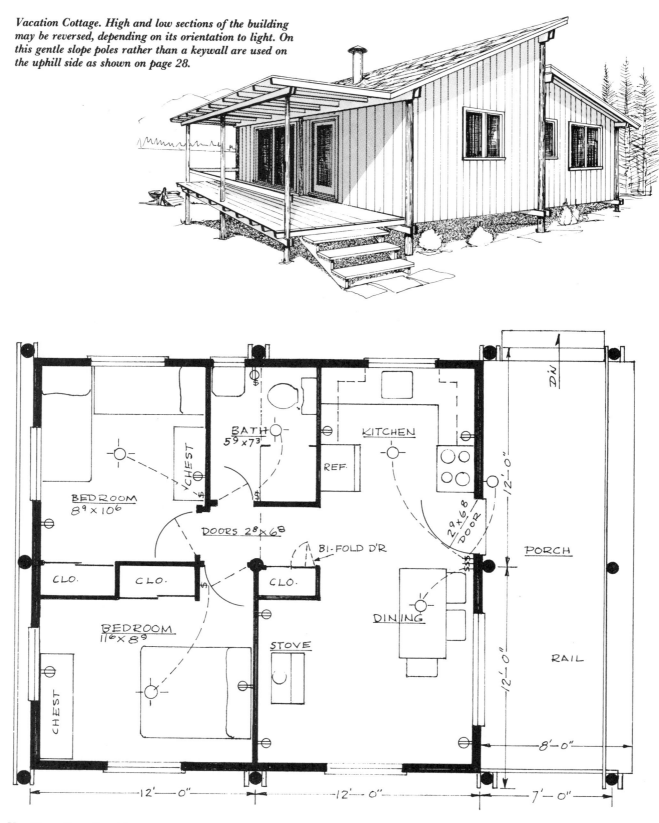

Vacation cottage floor plan.

Vacation Cottage

This cottage has been laid out to take advantage of standard construction lumber, which comes in increments of two feet. If you want to change the outside dimensions, keep this in mind, to avoid needless waste. In the plans it is essentially square—less the porch.

One modification of previous text instructions is very important: Because of the natural taper of poles, it is difficult to enclose them in walls. So in this and the following designs the poles are left *outside* the building proper. The poles must be set vertical to the *inside* face rather than the outside.

One of the advantages of a pole building is that none of the walls is load-bearing, so that the partitions and even outside walls can be changed at will without affecting the basic structure. The sequence of building would be: poles erected, girders attached at eaves and floor levels, followed by joists, rafters, roofing and flooring. At this stage you have a solid platform sheltered by a roof. Walls and partitions now can be constructed on this platform out of the elements.

Modifications to be considered might include eliminating the clerestory windows by raising or dropping the peak at the center line of the building, though this would diminish the ventilation and light which such windows provide.

All studding (2×4s) is two feet on centers to take advantage of the standard four-foot width of most plywood and paneling. Window sizes are suggested only, and accurate rough opening sizes should be checked when ordering windows. Any of various siding materials can be used, and insulation and inside finish can be added at your convenience.

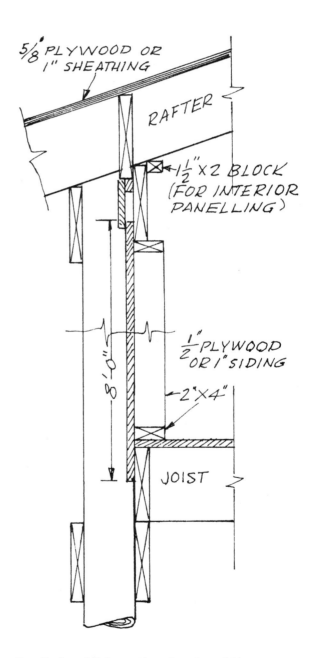

Details A and B for section view, page 144.

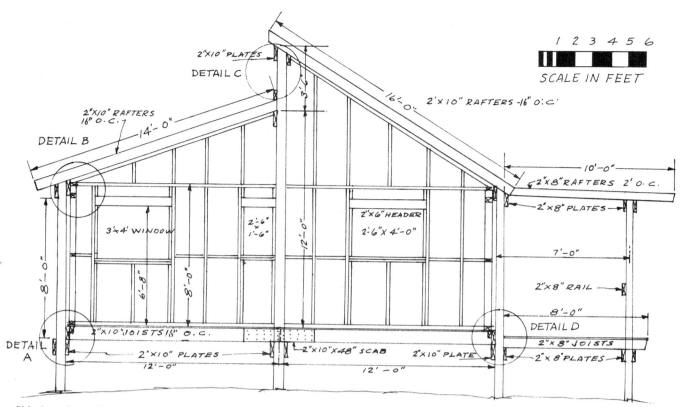

SCALE IN FEET
1 2 3 4 5 6

2"X10" PLATES
DETAIL C
2"X10" RAFTERS 16" O.C.
DETAIL B
14'-0"
2"X10" RAFTERS 16" O.C.
3'-2"
16'-0"
2"X10" RAFTERS -16" O.C.
10'-0"
2"X8" RAFTERS 2' O.C.
2"X8" PLATES
3'x4' WINDOW
2'-6" x 1'-6"
2"X6" HEADER
2'6"X4'-0"
12'-0"
7'-0"
8'-0"
6'-8"
8'-0"
2"X8" RAIL
8'-0"
DETAIL D
DETAIL A
2"X10" JOISTS 15" O.C.
2"X8" JOISTS
2"X10" PLATES
12'-0"
2"X10"X48" SCAB
2"X10" PLATE
12'-0"
2"X8" JOISTS
2"X8" PLATES

Sideview of vacation cottage. Insulation of the cottage for off-season use would require application of batts under roof sheathing or, if planned for during building, insulating plank sheathing.

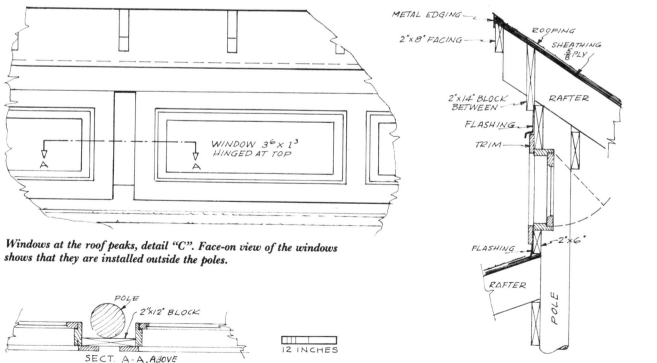

WINDOW 3⁶×1³
HINGED AT TOP

A   A

Windows at the roof peaks, detail "C". Face-on view of the windows shows that they are installed outside the poles.

METAL EDGING
2"X8" FACING
ROOFING
SHEATHING ⅝ PLY
2"X14" BLOCK BETWEEN
RAFTER
FLASHING
TRIM
FLASHING
2"X6"
RAFTER
POLE

POLE
2"X12" BLOCK

12 INCHES

SECT. A-A, ABOVE

This sectional view shows in detail how windows bridge around central pole.

Side view of the windows indicates arrangement of roof flashings above and below the windows.

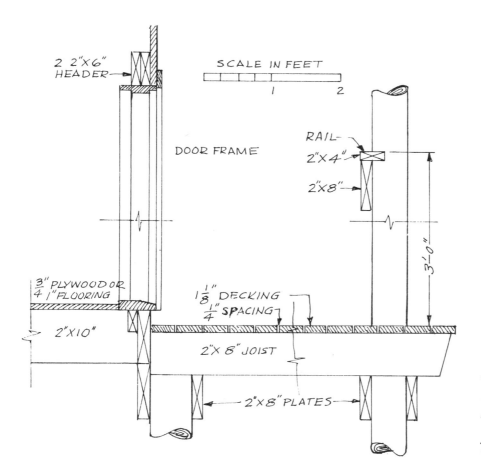

2 2"X6"
HEADER

SCALE IN FEET

1   2

DOOR FRAME

RAIL
2"X4"

2"X8"

3'-0"

$\frac{3}{4}$" PLYWOOD OR
$\frac{1}{4}$ 1" FLOORING

$1\frac{1}{8}$" DECKING
$\frac{1}{4}$" SPACING

2"X10"

2"X 8" JOIST

2"X8" PLATES

Vacation cottage porch. Here in detail "D," taken from side view on page 144, is the cottage porch, hung at a slightly lower level than the main floor.

When building exterior porches or decks, the use of naturally resistant woods, or even better, the use of pressure-treated lumber for both the deck boards and floor joists will avoid much maintenance and later grief.

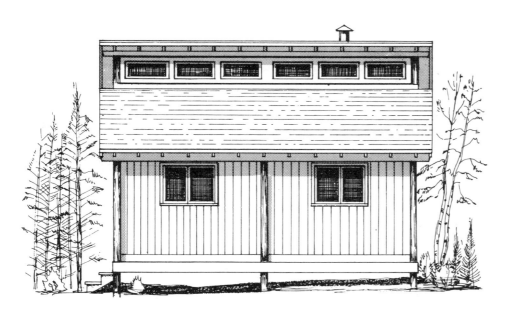

Rear view of vacation cottage. High windows between the staggered roof ridges may be hinged to open for ventilation by remote connections.

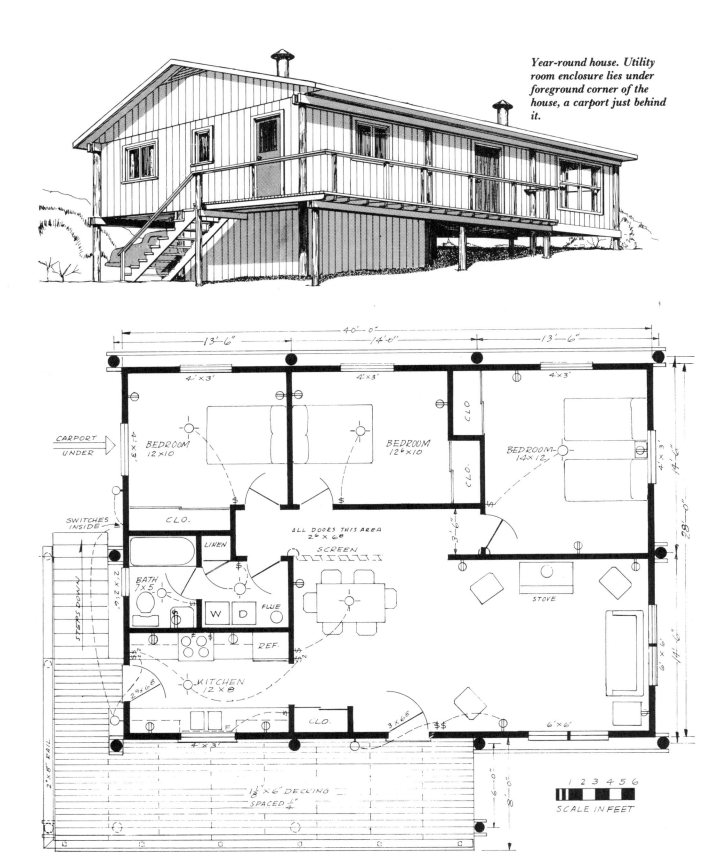

Year-round house. Utility room enclosure lies under foreground corner of the house, a carport just behind it.

CARPORT
UNDER

BEDROOM
12 x 10

4'x3'

BEDROOM
12'6"x10'

4'x3'

BEDROOM
14 x 12

4'x3'

CLO.

CLO.

CLO.

SWITCHES
INSIDE

CLO.

LINEN

ALL DOORS THIS AREA
2'6" X 6'8"

SCREEN

STEPS DOWN

2" X 2'6"

BATH
7 x 5

W   D   FLUE

STOVE

2'0 X 6'8

REF.

KITCHEN
12 X 8

CLO.

3 X 6'8

6'x6'

6'x6'

4'x3'

2' X 8" RAIL

1⅛"X 6" DECKING
SPACED ¼"

6'-0"

8'-0"

40'-0"

13'-6"   14'-0"   13'-6"

4'x3'

14'-6"

28'-0"

14'-6"

1 2 3 4 5 6
SCALE IN FEET

Floor plan of year-round house. Interior arrangement of the house is capable of many modifications. Note there are no interior support poles in this plan and center poles at ends reach to the floor plates only.

Year-Round House

Locating a pole building on a suitable slope can provide a dividend of a carport and a storage area, as shown in these drawings. This 28×40-foot house uses roof trusses to eliminate interior poles and thus achieves a spaciousness unusual for a relatively small house. Many lumberyards build standard trusses which, if purchased, would save a great deal of time and labor. If you want to do this part yourself, make a master pattern and follow it closely, so that each truss will be the same. It is important to use plenty of nails and to coat every joint with a resorcinol glue. Glue itself has become much more widely used in home construction, the flooring and wall paneling in particular being secured with glue as well as nails.

As with the vacation cottage, all walls and partitions are non load-bearing, and the plans can be modified easily to suit a family's needs. A major difference is the ground floor storage and furnace room, through which all water and drainage lines are run. Bathroom and kitchen are located above this room, and in colder climates a concrete foundation below the frost line would be advisable.

The roof may also be built of standard pole construction, replacing the roof trusses with rafters and ridge girders carried by tall interior poles. The house may be heated with wood-burning stoves or with a central heating system, as described earlier.

Required above the wood, gas or oil furnace are two plenums or chambers, one for the hot air feed and the other for the cold air return. From these plenums come the main rectangular ducts (8×16 inches). At the appropriate places these ducts feed hot air into six-inch diameter pipes, located between the joists, which supply hot air to each room. These ducts terminate in 90° boots topped with supply registers located as close as possible to the outside walls. Each of these feeder ducts should be equipped with a damper to regulate air flow.

The cold air return ducts are located in or near the interior walls and are formed by enclosing the bottom of a pair of joists with sheet metal pans, as shown in the drawing. Six-inch pipe can be used instead, if preferred, here also. The passages above the cold air ducts are blocked off with lengths of 2×10s. Note that the living room cold air duct is carried to the ceiling height between a pair of studs, while the kitchen and bath share a common cold air return. Both the hot and cold air ducts should be insulated as heavily as possible to minimize heat loss.

The plan may be slightly modified to provide a closet for the furnace and water heater, thus eliminating the need for a furnace room below the floor. And if a hot-water heating system with boiler is used instead of a furnace, bulky air ducts may be replaced with small pipes and fin-tube baseboard heating units.

How much of your own electrical work you can do is usually governed by the local building code. Some areas require that all electrical work be done by a licensed electrician while others have

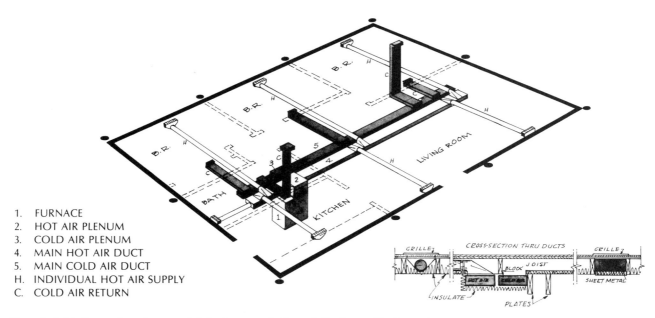

1. FURNACE
2. HOT AIR PLENUM
3. COLD AIR PLENUM
4. MAIN HOT AIR DUCT
5. MAIN COLD AIR DUCT
H. INDIVIDUAL HOT AIR SUPPLY
C. COLD AIR RETURN

Forced air heating system. Large metal ducts carry air through the house. Ducts must run below or between floor joists and girders, heavily insulated to avoid heat loss in winter.

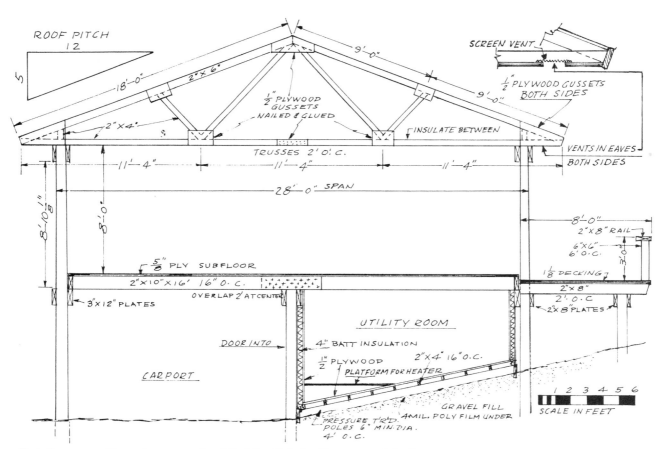

End of year-round house in cross-section. The 28 x 40-foot ceiling area and the floor area (less the utility room section) are heavily insulated for winter comfort and fuel economy.

End view of year-round house.
Door at top of stairs enters kitchen.
Living room main entrance is
around corner of the deck.

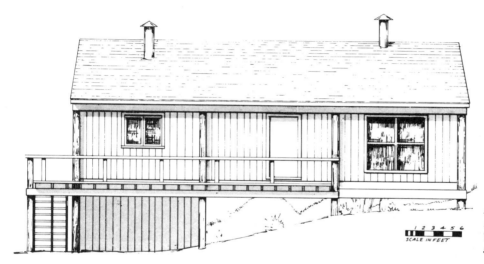

Entrance side of year-round house.
Roof stack at left connects to furnace.
The one at right is for supplementary
stove or free-standing fireplace.

no code and use the standards set by the National Electric Code. Similarly some codes specify armored cable (metal-sheathed BX) while others permit the use of plastic covered Romex cable.

For the year-round house an entrance service panel is located in the utility room with at least six branch circuits and three spares. Switches are generally located forty-two inches from the floor and duplex outlets fifteen inches from the floor except in the kitchen and bathroom where they should be located at a convenient height. Strip outlets against the wall over the kitchen counter are convenient for multiple use. Electric stoves and dryers need 220-volt outlets. Outdoor fixtures should be weatherproof and generally use

cast aluminum lamp holders with 150 watt outdoor floodlamps. Following is an explanation of symbols used in the floor plans for the Vacation Cottage and two year-round homes.

S	Switch	⊖	Duplex outlet
S_2	Two way switch	⌐⊖	Outlet with switch
⊙	Wall fixture	F	Fluorescent fixture
⊙	Ceiling fixture	_ _ _	Connecting cable

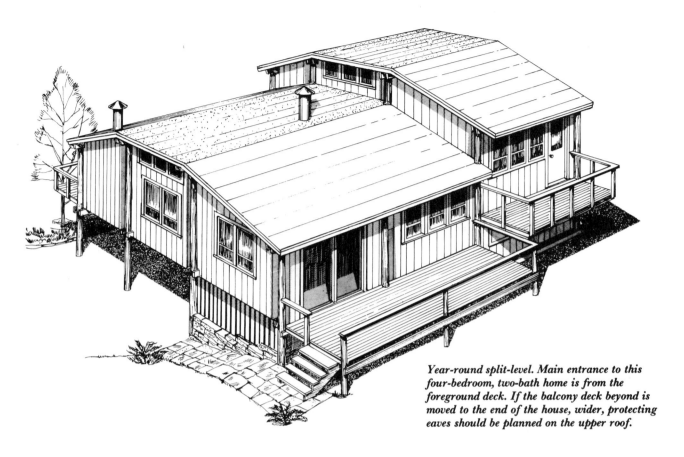

Year-round split-level. Main entrance to this four-bedroom, two-bath home is from the foreground deck. If the balcony deck beyond is moved to the end of the house, wider, protecting eaves should be planned on the upper roof.

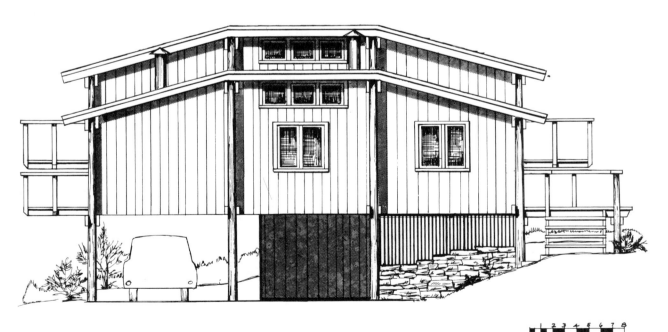

SCALE

End view of split-level. Upper balconies shown here attach to the upper, corner bedrooms. The clerestory windows between the roof levels light the central stairways. The utility room at lower center is recessed fourteen feet from the near wall.

Split-Level House

This 36×38-foot year-round house, the largest and most ambitious project in these building plans, provides for 1700 square feet of living space. It is distinguished by clerestory windows in the living room and at the top of the stairwell. The living room and both upper level rooms have balconies.

A further refinement is the centrally-located utility room's masonry foundation (with concrete block or poured walls), which is shown in the Cross Section and also in the Lower Level Floor Plan following. These two plans also show the stairway entrance to the utility room. Entry to living areas is provided by a sliding door off the main deck (see top left area of the Floor Plan).

Plumbing and heating appliances and connections for the house are contained in the utility room, and the chimney flue runs through a corner of the kitchen. A heating duct diagram is not included here, but could be planned in similar fashion to that shown with the preceding Year-Round House Plan. The use of baseboard hot water heating is recommended, however, for ease of installation.

Procedures for construction follow the main text generally. The outside poles should be trued up on their *inside* faces.

If you wish to avoid the trouble and expense of laying a concrete foundation, the utility room may be omitted. Enlarge one of the closets to house the furnace or boiler, and place a door at the head of the stairs leading from the carport below.

In these plans all the floor joists are connected to the girders by manufactured metal joist

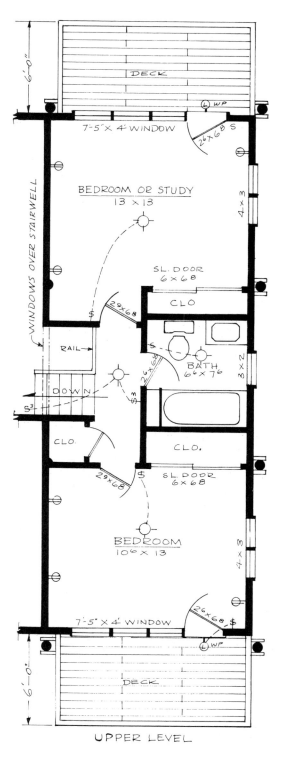

UPPER LEVEL

Split-level house — upper floor plan. There also is direct entrance to the house from below — from the carport area via the utility room, as shown also in Cross-Section view on page 155. If the terrain permits, tool or fuel storage may be planned at the end of the utility room.

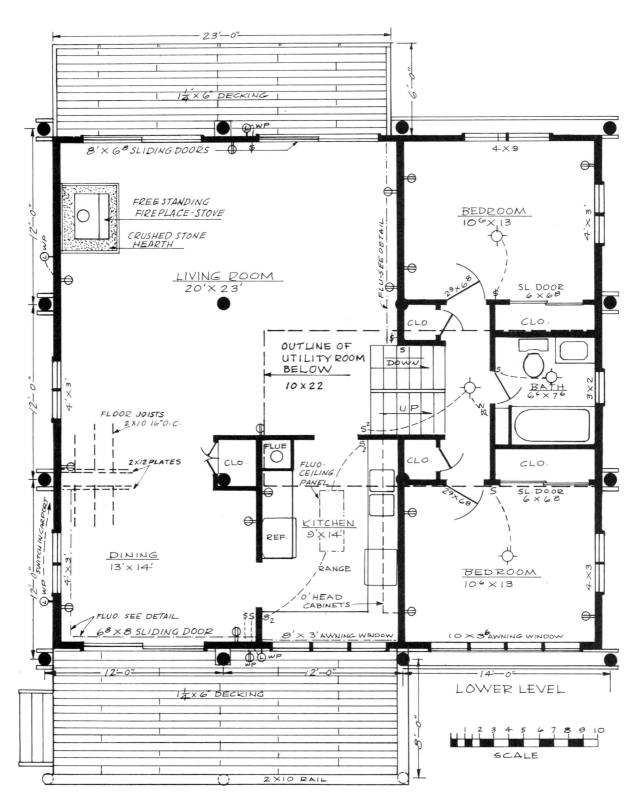

23'-0"

1¼" X 6" DECKING

6'-0"

8' X 6⁸ SLIDING DOORS

4 X 3

L. WP

FREE STANDING
FIREPLACE-STOVE

CRUSHED STONE
HEARTH

BEDROOM
10⁶ X 13

12'-0"

WP

4'X 3'

LIVING ROOM
20' X 23'

SL. DOOR
6 X 6⁸

CLO.

29 X 6⁸

CLO.

OUTLINE OF
UTILITY ROOM
BELOW
10 X 22

S
DOWN

BATH
6⁶ X 7⁶

S

3 X 2

UP

FLOOR JOISTS
2 X 10 16" O.C.

FLUE

CLO.

2 X 12 PLATES

FLUO.
CEILING
PANEL

CLO.

12'-0"

4' X 3'

12'-0"
SWITCH IN CARPORT

WP

DINING
13' X 14'

KITCHEN
9' X 14'

REF.

29 X 6⁸

S

SL. DOOR
6 X 6⁸

BEDROOM
10⁶ X 13

4 X 3

RANGE

O' HEAD
CABINETS

4'X 3'

FLUO. SEE DETAIL

6⁸ X 8 SLIDING DOOR

$ S 8²

8' X 3' AWNING WINDOW

10 X 3⁶ AWNING WINDOW

WP

12'-0"

12'-0"

14'-0"

1¼" X 6" DECKING

LOWER LEVEL

8'-0"

2 X 10 RAIL

1 2 3 4 5 6 7 8 9 10
SCALE

Split-level house — lower level plan.

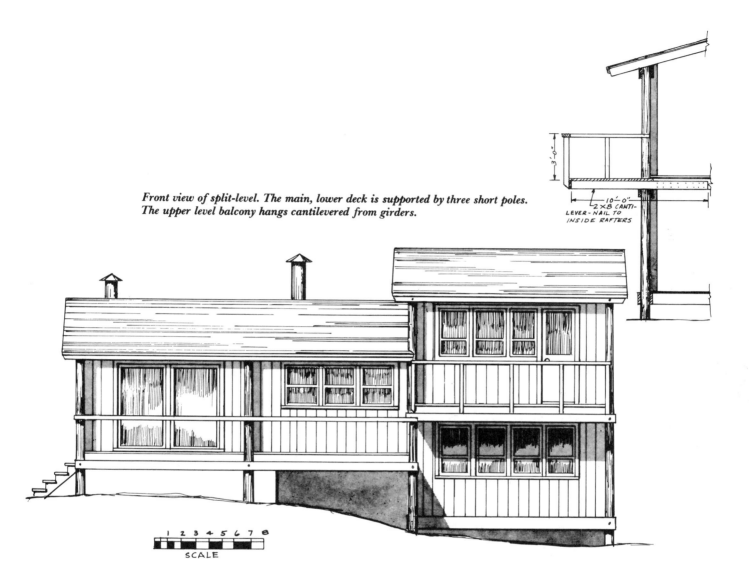

Front view of split-level. The main, lower deck is supported by three short poles. The upper level balcony hangs cantilevered from girders.

hangers except where the upper decks or hanging balconies occur. So that these balcony joists will be cantilevered, the girders at these points are lowered the width of the joists, rather than being flush—as shown in the Balcony Detail view.

Because of the flat surfaces of the roofs, built-up gravel surfaced roofing should be planned there. Heavier than usual roof rafters and upper girders are used to allow for the extra weight of this roofing and snow load. Pole spacing is twelve feet.

In northern climates the roof areas, as well as side walls and floors, should be heavily insulated. The furnace for this house, when built for severe winters, should have a 160,000 BTU capacity. The electric service entrance panel, located in the utility room, should be of the 200 amperes size.

Since none of the walls of the house is load-bearing, the wall studs could be located twenty-four inches on center rather than the usual sixteen inches. This would save materials and labor. The floor joists, however, should be kept at sixteen inches on center.

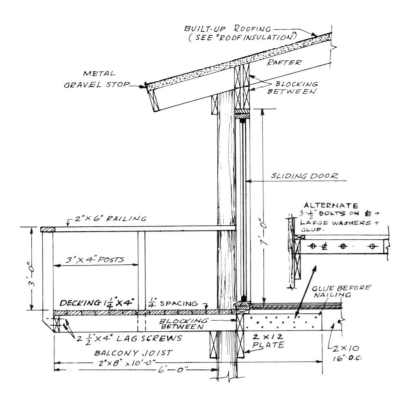

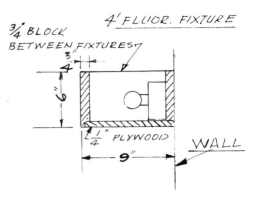

Indirect lighting. Standard fluorescent strips may be boxed as in this detail plan for use along an interior wall of the living room, as indicated in the floor plan on page 152.

Balcony detail for split-level. Like the higher bedroom balconies, the deck off the living room area hangs cantilevered as an extension of the floor joists.

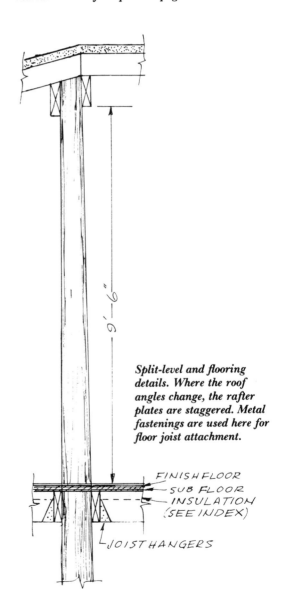

Split-level and flooring details. Where the roof angles change, the rafter plates are staggered. Metal fastenings are used here for floor joist attachment.

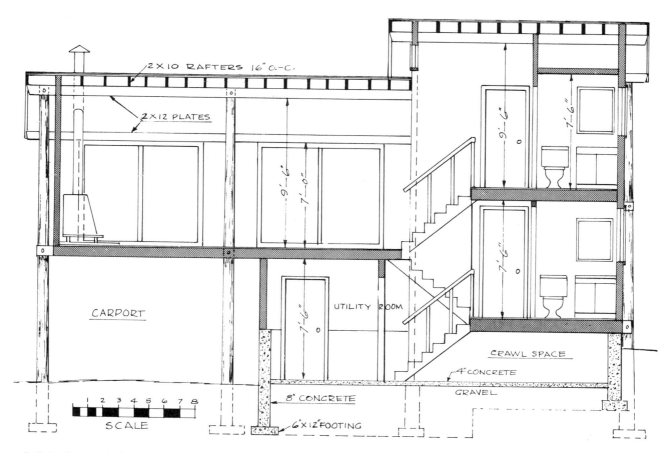

2X10 RAFTERS 16" O.C.

2X12 PLATES

9'-6"

7'-0"

9'-6"

7'-6"

7'-6"

CARPORT

7'-6"

UTILITY ROOM

CRAWL SPACE

4" CONCRETE

GRAVEL

8" CONCRETE

6"X12" FOOTING

1 2 3 4 5 6 7 8

SCALE

*Split-level cross-section. Stairs in house center reach up to small upper hall, down to
similar hall on lower sleeping level, and further down to the utility room and carport level.
Or eliminate utility room, and place door at head of stairs from carport.*

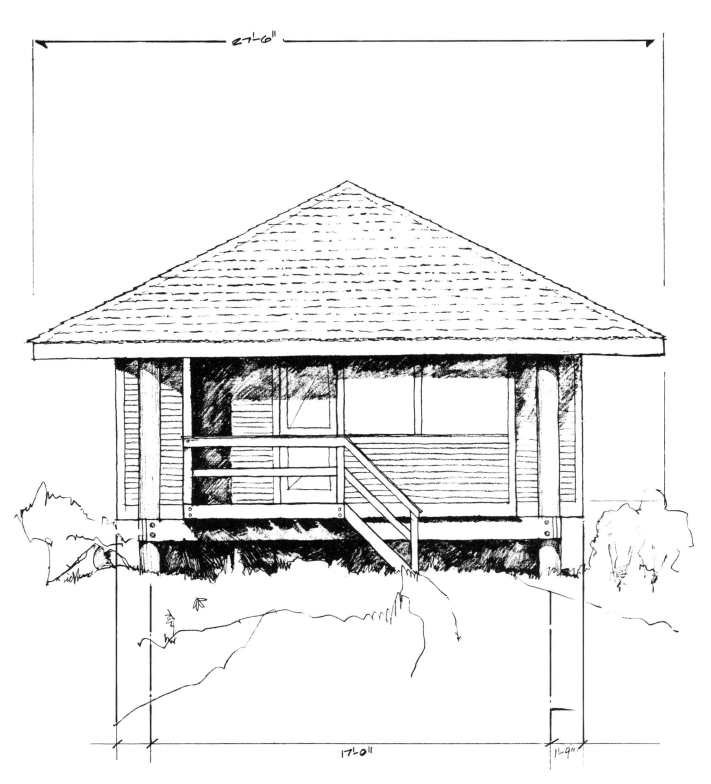

Front elevation — Camp Cabin 1.

Camp Cabin 1

This little cabin, designed by first-year architecture students at Yale, combines utter simplicity with a subtle reference to Japanese articulation. The square-hipped roof stands on four corner poles; screened windows open on all four sides, giving the effect of a floating canopy in the forest.

The cabin was originally designed to accommodate seven bunk beds, but is easily adapted for use as a modest vacation shelter. For year-round living, the cabin may be insulated and equipped with a wood-burning stove (on a flagstone base, please). The screened shutters may be replaced by windows of insulating glass.

The four corner poles stand about twelve feet above grade. Double girders are bolted to the outside of the poles. Then 2×12 diagonal floor joists are installed, either notched into the poles or hung from joist hangers. They are supported at the center by a fifth, short pole. Next, the floor joists are cantilevered from the diagonals out over the girders. (Make sure to install the 2×12 diagonals at the correct height so that the top edges are even with the smaller joists which frame into them.)

The radiating pattern of floor joists below produces a parquet-type pattern when the floorboards are installed.

To build the roof, use a tall stepladder or temporary scaffolding to support the peak. Install the hip-rafters first, then the other rafters. After they are in place, mark them with a string to trim them off evenly. Then install the fascia: it will need to be in two pieces, so splice it with a steel strap for strength. Fasten the roof down securely to the poles and girders to prevent wind damage.

Side elevation — Camp Cabin 1.

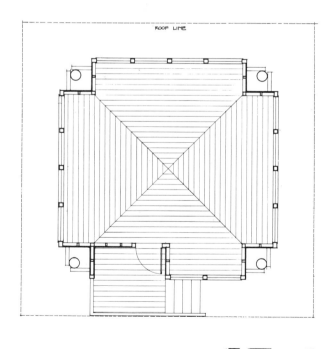

Plan — Camp Cabin 1.

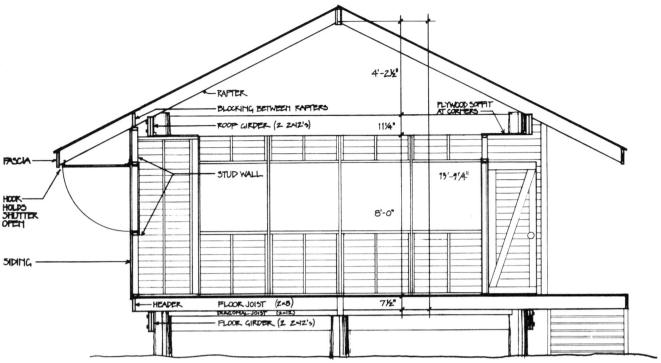

Section — Camp Cabin 1.

The roof may be sheathed with plywood. If you'd like a colored ceiling, paint or stain the plywood *before* nailing it to the roof; it's much easier than painting it later.

With the roof overhead to protect against the rain, the walls may be assembled on the platform floor, then tilted up into place. The walls may be sheathed with 1×6 tongue-and-groove cedar siding, as shown. Make the door and the shutters out of the same material. Be sure to use treated wood where the steps hit the ground.

Materials List — Camp Cabin 1

Please note that this list is only approximate. Use it to obtain an approximate materials cost from your local lumberyard, then re-calculate everything before ordering to avoid waste.

POLES:		4 @ 18 ft. (varies) × 12″
		1 @ 8 ft. (varies) × 12″
FLOOR:	Girders:	8 2×12's @ 18 ft. (All structural lumber is Douglas fir #2)
	Joists:	4 2×12's @ 12 ft.
		2 2×8's @ 14 ft.
		11 2×8's @ 10 ft.
		12 2×8's @ 8 ft.
		8 2×8's @ 6 ft.
	Flooring:	500 ft² of 1×6 T&G spruce
ROOF:	Girders:	8 2×12's @ 18 ft.

Rafters:	4 2×8's @ 20 ft.
	24 2×8's @ 16 ft.
Fascia:	8 2×10's @ 14 ft.
Sheathing:	32 pieces ⅝″ exterior plyscore or plywood
	5 rolls roofing felt — 1000 ft²
	30 bundles of asphalt shingles
WALLS:	Approximately 500 linear ft. of 2×4's
	4 4×4's @ 8 ft.
	Approx. 900 ft² of 1×6
OTHER:	Concrete for footings
	Stain for siding, ceiling
	Bolts or lag screws
	Roofing nails
	Flooring nails
	Common nails for walls

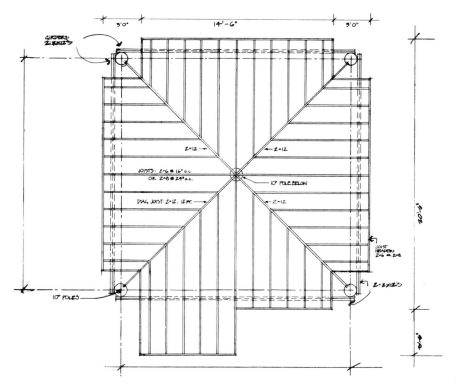

Floor framing — Camp Cabin 1.

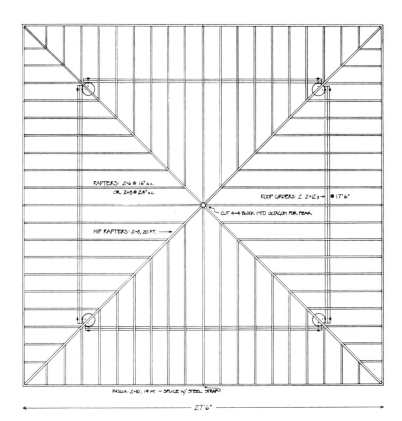

Roof framing — Camp Cabin 1.

Camp Cabin 2 features a large monitor window for light and ventilation.

Photo by Will Paxson

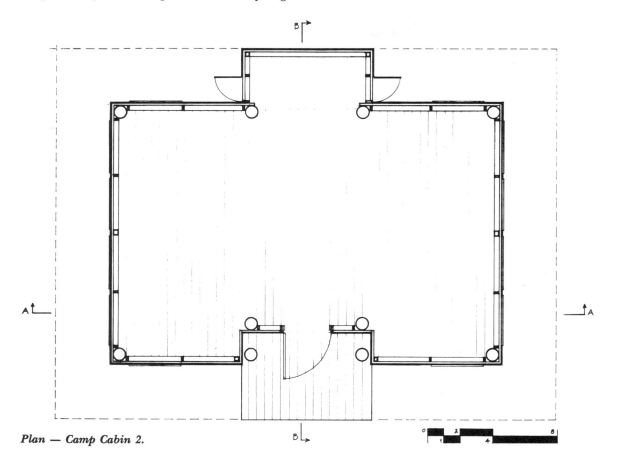

Plan — Camp Cabin 2.

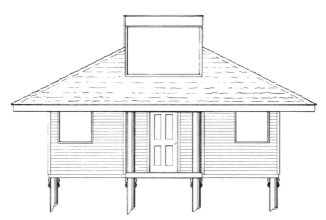

Front elevation — Camp Cabin 2.

Camp Cabin 2

Here is another elegant little cabin, this one also adapted from a design by Yale architecture students. The 380 square-foot one-room building features a large high window for sunlight, warmth, and ventilation. The plan is based on an eight-foot module to maximize efficient use of lumber. Like Camp Cabin 1, this cottage may be winterized for year-round use.

The cabin stands on ten poles: eight of them at about twelve feet above grade, and two which reach up another seven feet or so to frame the high window. (Pole lengths are approximate, and vary with the slope of the land. Use poles several feet longer than necessary, and trim after the roof is framed. Don't be caught short.) Plumb the outside faces of the poles, add the floor and roof girders, and fill in the holes.

The floor framing uses a system of overlapping joists which may be used just as they come from the lumberyard, without need for trimming. Be sure to insert blocking or cross-bridging between the joists to support them.

To frame the roof, start with the **five** longest rafters—the ones which reach up to the high poles. Then add the hip rafters and the shorter rafters. Trim the rafter ends once they are in place, and install the fascia. A scaffold makes this job easier.

The walls are built of wall girts attached to the outsides of the poles. At four places, the wall turns a corner without touching a pole; use a 4×4 stud at each of these corners, nailed into the rafter above.

Make shutters out of the siding material, such as 1×6 tongue-and-groove cedar siding. A quick

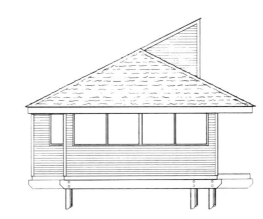

Side elevation — Camp Cabin 2.

way to do this: frame the walls for the shutters, then apply the siding to the whole wall, covering over the window openings. Then cut out the shutter openings with a Skil-saw, after attaching z-shaped reinforcing boards to each shutter. This method is a little tricky, but it produces perfectly matched shutters. To locate the exact corners of the shutters on the outside for cutting, drill or nail a small hole through from within. This job should be done by someone very experienced with a Skil-saw; otherwise, use a hand saw or make the shutters some other, safer way.

The alcove at the rear could accommodate a double bed, or a kitchenette. The shutters may be hooked open all summer, making this little cabin into a cool and breezy screened pavilion in the woods.

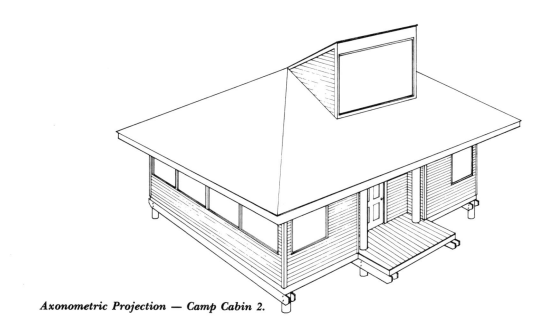

Axonometric Projection — Camp Cabin 2.

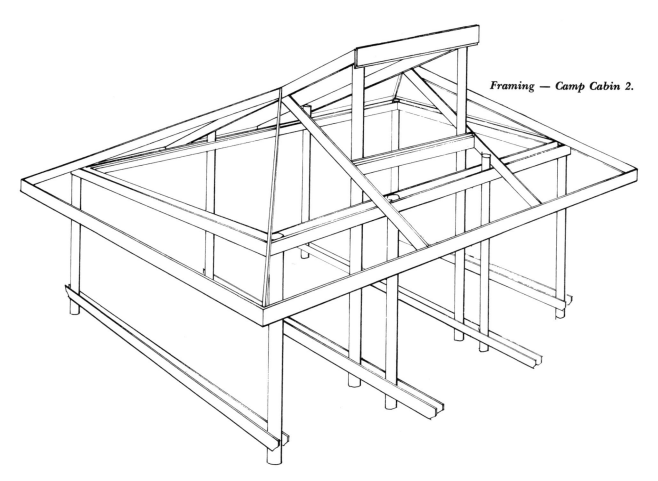

Framing — Camp Cabin 2.

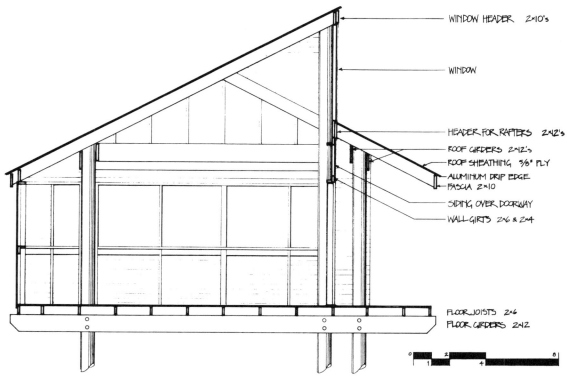

WINDOW HEADER 2×10's

WINDOW

HEADER FOR RAFTERS 2×12's
ROOF GIRDERS 2×12's
ROOF SHEATHING ⅝" PLY
ALUMINUM DRIP EDGE
FASCIA 2×10
SIDING OVER DOORWAY
WALL GIRTS 2×6 & 2×4

FLOOR JOISTS 2×6
FLOOR GIRDERS 2×12

Section A — Camp Cabin 2.

Section B — Camp Cabin 2.

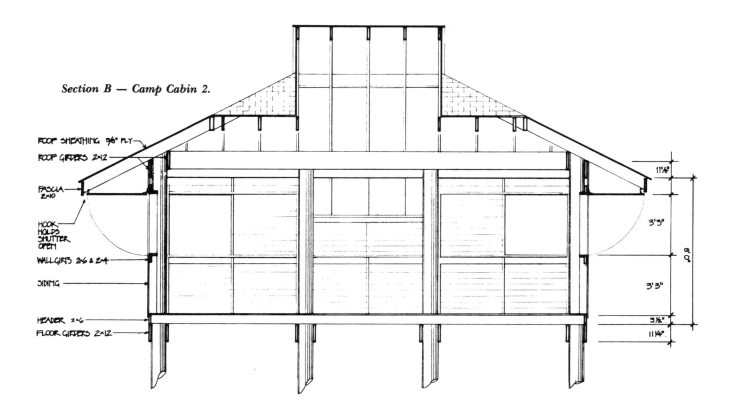

ROOF SHEATHING ⅝" PLY

ROOF GIRDERS 2×12

FASCIA
2×10

HOOK
HOLDS
SHUTTER
OPEN

WALL GIRTS 2×6 & 2×4

SIDING

HEADER 2×6

FLOOR GIRDERS 2×12

11¼"

3'3"

3'3"

5½"

11¼"

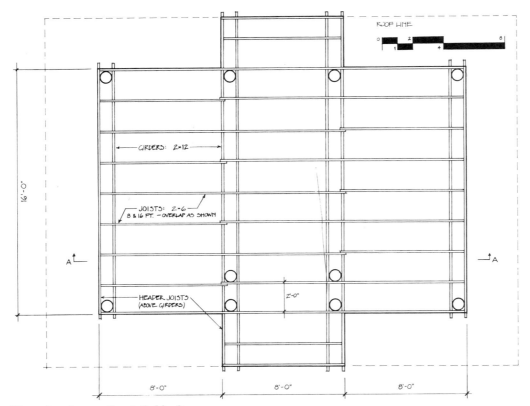

Floor framing — Camp Cabin 2.

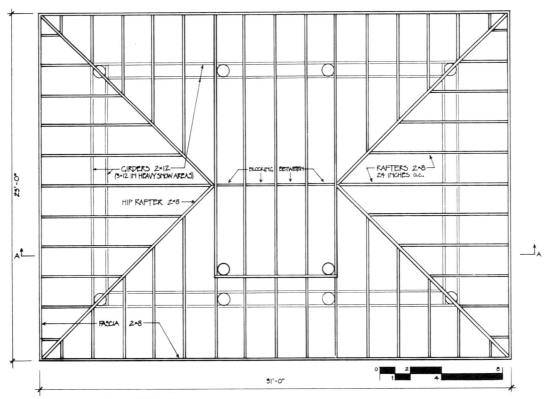

Roof framing — Camp Cabin 2.

Materials List: Camp Cabin 2

Please note: lumber prices vary widely, and invariably rise. So it is impossible to include an accurate estimate of costs in this book. Use this rough list of materials to obtain an approximate price from your local lumberyard. Then go back and recalculate all quantities more precisely, to avoid waste.

POLES:
- 8 @ 18 ft. (varies) × 12″
- 2 @ 25 ft. (varies) × 12″

FLOOR:

Girders:
- 4 2×12's @ 18 ft. (All structural lumber is Douglas fir #2)
- 4 2×12's @ 24 ft.

Joists:
- 11 2×6's @ 16 ft.
- 13 2×6's @ 8 ft.

Flooring:
- 500 ft² of 1×6 T&G spruce

ROOF:

Girders:
- 4 2×12's @ 16 ft.
- 4 2×12's @ 24 ft.; or 4 @ 16 ft., 4 @ 8 ft. (splice)

Rafters:
- 5 2×8's @ 20 ft.
- 4 2×8's @ 18 ft.
- 4 2×8's @ 14 ft.
- 8 2×8's @ 12 ft.
- 8 2×8's @ 10 ft.
- 17 2×8's @ 8 ft.

Headers:
- 2 2×12's @ 8 ft.
- 2 2×10's @ 8 ft.

Fascia:
- 10 2×10's @ 12 ft.

Sheathing:
- 32 pieces ⅝″ exterior plyscore or plywood
- 5 rolls roofing felt — 1000 ft²
- 30 bundles of asphalt shingles

WALLS:
- 46 2×4's @ 8 ft.
- 6 4×4's @ 8 ft.
- 20 2×6 @ 8 ft.
- Approximately 1000 ft² of 1×6 T&G cedar siding

OTHER:
- Concrete for footings
- Stain for siding, ceiling
- Bolts or lag screws
- Roofing nails
- Flooring nails
- Common nails for walls
- Metal fasteners
- Hardware for door, shutters
- Window screen

Optional:
- Insulation
- Polyethylene vapor barrier
- Windows

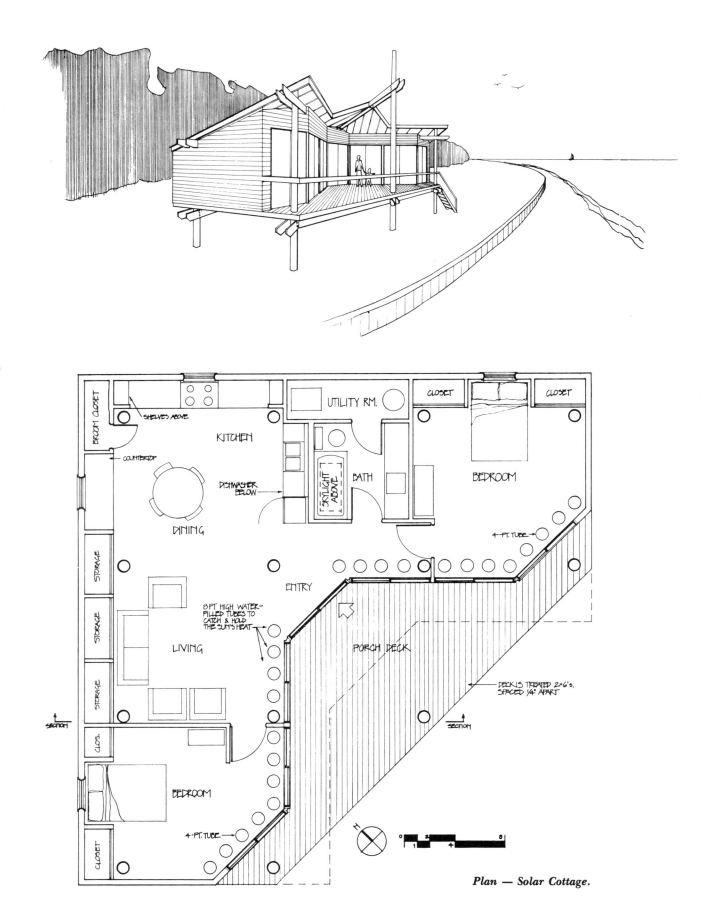

BROOM CLOSET

SHELVES ABOVE

KITCHEN

COUNTERTOP

DISHWASHER BELOW

UTILITY RM.

CLOSET

CLOSET

SKYLIGHT ABOVE

BATH

BEDROOM

STORAGE

DINING

4-FT. TUBE

STORAGE

STORAGE

ENTRY

8-FT. HIGH WATER-FILLED TUBES TO CATCH & HOLD THE SUN'S HEAT

LIVING

PORCH DECK

DECK IS TREATED 2×6's, SPACED 1/4" APART

SECTION

CLOS.

SECTION

BEDROOM

4-FT. TUBE

CLOSET

N

0   2   8
  1   4

Plan — Solar Cottage.

Solar Cottage

The sun is the furnace for this two-bedroom pole house. Depending on the local climate, this passive-solar design will derive 50 to 75 percent of its heating from the sun, without expensive technological gadgets or exotic plumbing.

The key element of the design is the waterwall: a row of translucent water-filled tubes just inside the sliding glass doors which line the south face of the house. These tubes collect and hold the sun's heat in winter, retaining their warmth through the night and greatly reducing the need for supplementary heat. At night, insulating drapes are pulled across the windows to reduce heat loss. The north sides have only a few small windows, and the roof line drops down to deflect cold north winds up and over. In addition, the entire northeast and northwest walls are lined with closets to further buffer against the cold, as well as to provide ample storage in lieu of a basement.

All the plumbing is consolidated, to reduce costs and minimize vulnerable under-floor piping runs. The plan provides a utility room for a water heater and the boiler, if oil or gas is used as the backup fuel source. In that case, a forced-hot-water heating system is recommended. If wood-burning stoves are to provide backup heat, eliminate the utility room, or use it as a laundry room.

The 1000 square-foot house has a large porch deck on the sunny south side. Entry to the house is from the porch; it is set in to protect against chilly winds. In summer, all the sliding glass doors may be opened for ventilation. A few of the waterwall tubes may be short, to allow better views in a few strategic places.

Kalwall Corporation of Manchester, New

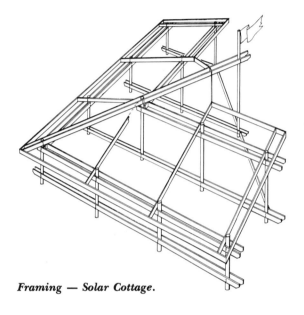

Framing — Solar Cottage.

Hampshire, manufactures fiberglass tubes for this purpose in various sizes and lengths. In 1978, eight-foot tubes twelve inches in diameter sold for $37 each. They are available as translucent, half-black or black. The black are most efficient as collectors, but the translucency is much nicer aesthetically, as the sunlight filters through the big pipe-organ columns. Or use metal irrigation pipe lined with a plastic liner. The pipe is cheap, and a waterbed maker will make the plastic liners inexpensively.

Because this solar house is not designed for a specific climate, it is based on rough rule-of-thumb design assumptions. In the Boston area, for example, the system should attain approximately 40 to 60 percent solar heating. For more information on passive solar house design, see *Home Energy for the Eighties,* by Ralph Wolfe and Peter Clegg (Garden Way, 1979).

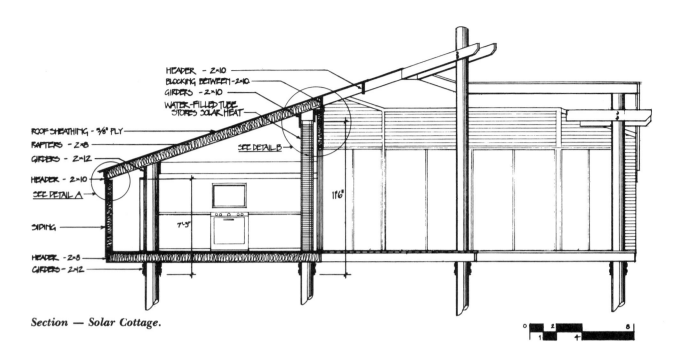

HEADER – 2×10
BLOCKING BETWEEN–2×10
GIRDERS – 2×10
WATER-FILLED TUBE
STORES SOLAR HEAT

ROOF SHEATHING – 3/8" PLY
RAFTERS – 2×8
GIRDERS – 2×12
HEADER – 2×10
SEE DETAIL A

SEE DETAIL B

11'6"

SIDING

7'3"

HEADER – 2×8
GIRDERS – 2×12

Section — Solar Cottage.

0   2   8
  1   4

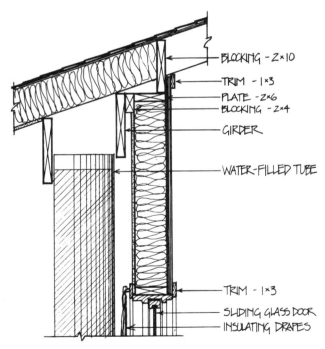

BLOCKING – 2×10
TRIM – 1×3
PLATE – 2×6
BLOCKING – 2×4

GIRDER

WATER-FILLED TUBE

TRIM – 1×3
SLIDING GLASS DOOR
INSULATING DRAPES

Detail A.

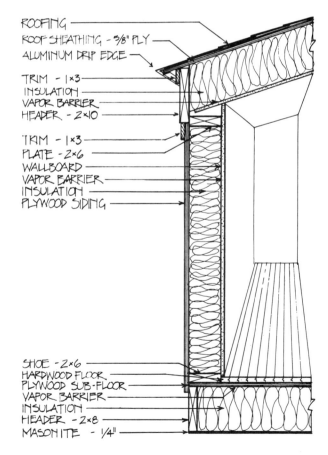

ROOFING
ROOF SHEATHING – 3/8" PLY
ALUMINUM DRIP EDGE

TRIM – 1×3
INSULATION
VAPOR BARRIER
HEADER – 2×10

TRIM – 1×3
PLATE – 2×6
WALLBOARD
VAPOR BARRIER
INSULATION
PLYWOOD SIDING

SHOE – 2×6
HARDWOOD FLOOR
PLYWOOD SUB-FLOOR
VAPOR BARRIER
INSULATION
HEADER – 2×8
MASONITE – 1/4"

Detail B.

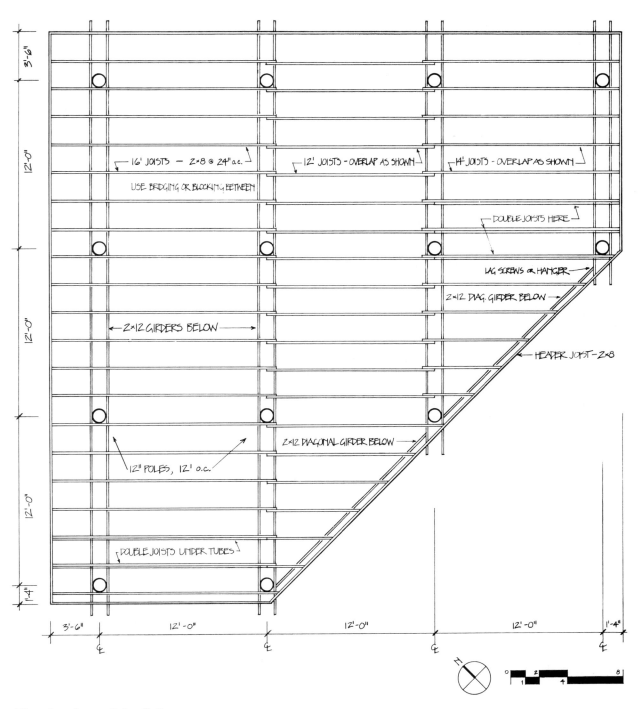

Floor framing — Solar Cottage.

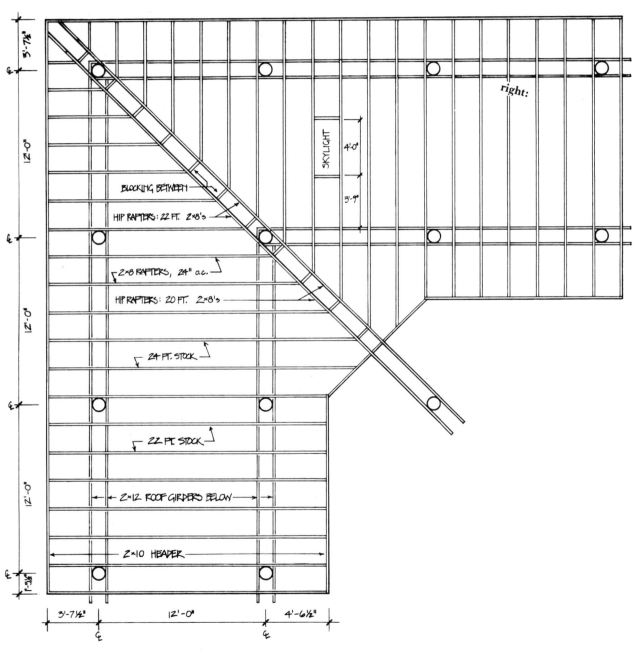

Roof framing — Solar Cottage.

Materials List: Solar Cottage

Please note that this is a rough estimate of quantities and lengths, to assist the reader in obtaining an approximate cost from the lumberyard. Be sure to recalculate all quantities and lengths more precisely before ordering, to reduce waste.

POLES:

7 @ 15 ft. (varies) × 12″

5 @ 20 ft. (varies) × 12″

1 @ 26 ft. (varies) × 12″

FLOOR: Girders: 2 2×12's @ 20 ft. (All structural lumber is Douglas fir #2)

8 @ 2×12's @ 16 ft.

4 2×12's @ 14 ft.

4 2×12's @ 12 ft.

Joists: 30 2×8's @ 16 ft.

17 2×8's @ 14 ft.

20 2×8's @ 12 ft.

Flooring: 1200 ft² of ⅝″ exterior plyscore (subfloor)

1200 ft² of T&G hardwood flooring

350 ft² of 2×6 for deck

1000 ft² of 7½″ fiberglass insulation, foil-faced

1200 ft² of masonite, ¼″, for underside of joists

ROOF: Girders: 12 2×12's @ 12 ft.

8 2×12's @ 14 ft.

Rafters: 4 2×8's @ 24 ft.

13 2×8's @ 22 ft.

5 2×8's @ 20 ft.

Fascia: 2 2×10's @ 16 ft.

4 2×10's @ 14 ft.

5 2×10's @ 12 ft.

Sheathing: 50 sheets ⅝″ plyscore or plywood

9 rolls of roofing felt — 1800 ft²

45 bundles of asphalt shingles

1400 ft² of 7½″ fiberglass insulation

1400 ft² of wallboard for ceiling (or use wood)

2×4 skylight for bathroom, operable

WALLS:

Approximately 700 ft. of 2×6

Approximately 800 ft. of 2×4

Approximately 1000 ft² of 1×6 T&G cedar siding

Approximately 800 ft² of 5½″ fiberglass insulation

7 sliding glass doors, 8 ft. high × 6 ft. wide

OTHER:

4 windows, approx. 30″×30″

Polyethylene vapor barrier

Caulking & weatherstripping

5 doors

Closet doors

22 10 ft. tubes, 2 4 ft. tubes

Interior wallboard: approximately 2400 ft² (wood or gypsum)

Floor tiles, counters, miscellaneous hardware

Water heater & furnace, with oil tank

Nails, bolts, fasteners

Concrete for footings

Stain or paint

Lighting fixtures

Kitchen equipment

Bathroom fixtures

Plumbing and electricity

Woodshed *is open to the south, protected by an ample roof overhang.*

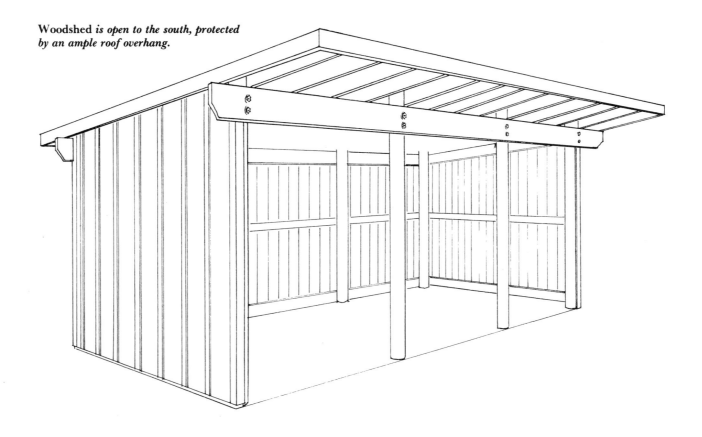

For a larger woodshed, extend the plan one or more eight-foot bays.

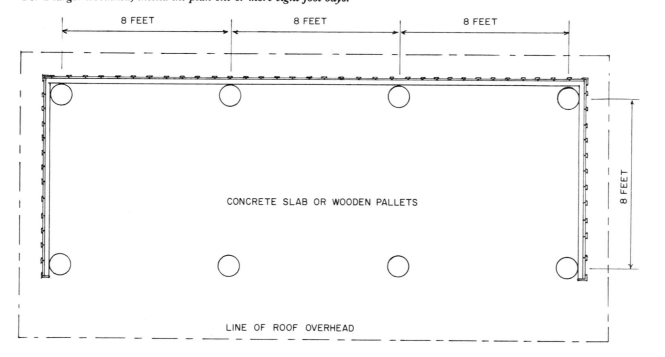

8 FEET   8 FEET   8 FEET

8 FEET

CONCRETE SLAB OR WOODEN PALLETS

LINE OF ROOF OVERHEAD

Woodshed

This simple shed has ample space inside for about eight cords of firewood; if you need more space, simply extend the plan for one or more additional eight-foot bays. The building is completely open on the south side, admitting sun and air to dry the wood as it seasons. Open construction at the eaves allows a free flow of air through the other three sides, too. Some will leave open all but the north side, for maximum ventilation.

Because termites are often present in cut firewood, use pressure-treated lumber for girts, splash boards, and siding. (For the same reason, it is wise not to bring more firewood inside your house than you plan to burn that day.) Pour a three-inch concrete floor slab, or construct a simple floor of 4×4 shipping pallets from a local factory. Use roll roofing rather than shingles, because of the low pitch of the roof.

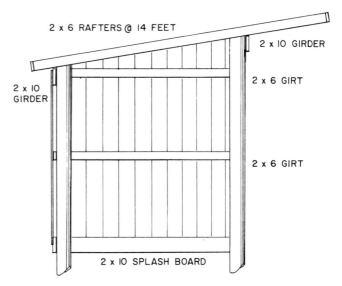

Woodshed *section. Leave an opening at the top of the wall below the eave to allow air flow.*

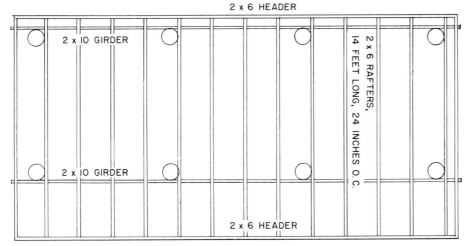

Roof framing.

Appendix 1

Suggested Tools for Pole Building

Axe or hatchet, for removing trees and brush, and for notching poles

Sledgehammer, for driving stakes and general persuasion

Carpenter's spirit level, the longer the better (four feet is good)

Plumb bob and string

Carpenter's twine, for guidelines and many other uses

Carpenter's Rafter square

Try square, a smaller version, less cumbersome for fine work

Chalk and carpenter's pencils

Claw hammer, I recommend a sixteen- or twenty-ounce curved-claw hammer

Carpenter's folding rule, for use when a rigid ruler is needed

Reel tape measure, 50 or 100 feet

20 ft. metal tape measure

Stepladder, 5 to 6 foot size is convenient for many tasks

Scaffolding and/or extension ladder, optional depending upon the height of the building. They can be rented.

Long-handled shovel

Post hole shovel, a must for pole construction. Sears sells one for $18.

Block and tackle with tripod, to maneuver heavy poles into place

Two adjustable or socket wrenches, for tightening bolts or screws. One should be long-handled for leverage.

High-strength threaded steel rod, used when squeezing the girder down against the spike grid. It is then replaced with a bolt.

Line level, cheap and fairly inaccurate, but okay for checking

20 ft. plastic tube, for an accurate level measurement

Chalk line, to mark joist location when nailing plywood, laying out roofing, etc.

"Cat's paw" nail puller; everybody makes mistakes

Electric drill, heavy duty, $\frac{1}{2}$ hp or larger, for bolt-holes

Bits (chisel or paddle type) to match lag screws or pre-bore for spikes or $\frac{1}{16}''$ larger than bolts, if used

(Alternate: hand brace and auger bits)

12″ bit extension for drill, to reach through the poles

Extension cord, heavy duty, 100 ft.

Chainsaw, to cut off pole ends

(Alternate: bucksaw)

Electric saw, for framing, plywood, etc.

(Alternate: hand saw, crosscut)

Hand chisel (one inch) and mallet, for miscellaneous trimming and
  shaving

Staple gun, for insulation, tar paper, polyethylene

Keyhole saw

Tin snips, for flashing

Caulking gun

Shears

Mat knife and blades

Carpenter's apron, for carrying nails, pencil, measure, etc.

The job is much easier when all blades are very sharp. They'll stay sharp
longer if each tool is used only for its intended job: don't use a chisel as a pry
bar, axe as a shovel, saws to cut nails, and so forth. Keep tools lightly oiled
and out of the rain, and they'll last a long time.

Appendix 2

Bibliography

Pole Building

American Institute of Timber Construction. *Timber Construction Manual.* New York: John Wiley & Son. Available in libraries. An engineer's reference, very technical.

American Wood Preservers Institute. *FHA Pole House Construction,* 2d ed. Greenfield, Ohio: Greenfield Publishing Co. 32 pages. Available free from AWPI, 1651 Old Meadow Road, McLean, VA 22101. A brief, well-illustrated introduction to pole buildings and FHA requirements.

J. H. Baxter Co. *Greenpole Homes.* 10 pages. Available free from J. H. Baxter Co., 1700 South El Camino Real, San Mateo, CA 94402. Baxter is one of the largest preservers of poles. This brief pamphlet contains plans and sketches of six pole houses, and ideas for several more.

Cornell University. *Pole Barn Construction.* Ithaca, N.Y.: Cornell University Press. Undated. Available as Bulletin no. 401.

Degenkolb, H. J. & Assoc. *Design Notes and Criteria — Pole Type Buildings.* 12 pages. Available free from AWPI, McLean, VA 22101. Brief and simple notes for engineers designing pole buildings. The interested layperson may find it fairly comprehensible.

Koppers Co., Inc., Koppers Building, Pittsburgh, PA 15219. The nation's largest manufacturer of wood preservatives, and a good source of information.

Lees, Alfred W. and Heyn, Ernest V. *Your Leisure Home.* Latham, NY: Popular Science Books, 1980. Contains updated versions of 20 articles on Lockbox pole house originally published 1972.

Lefer, Henry. "Protecting Wood From Its Enemies." *Progressive Architecture,* April 1977.

Norum, W. A. *Pole Buildings Go Modern.* Proceedings of the American Society of Civil Engineers, Journal of the Structural Division, April 1967.

Oregon State University Cooperative Extension Service. *Pole Type Structures.* 1968.

Patterson, Donald. *Pole Building Design.* AWPI, McLean, VA 22101. 1969. 48 pages. Available free from AWPI. Aimed at the engineer, partially readable by the layperson.

"Pole House in Sarasota, Florida." *Architectural Record,* November 1970, pp. 114-15.

"Pole House in Carmel, California." *Architectural Record,* Mid-May 1973, pp. 62-65.

"Pole house in Washington." *Architectural Record,* Mid-May, 1979.

Southern Forest Products Association. *How to Build Pole Type Frame Buildings.* New Orleans, LA. Undated.

"The Habitable Forest." (pole house in Connecticut) *Progressive Architecture,* Sept. 1968.

Vickers, Larry. "Our Florida Pole Barn House." *Mother Earth News* #26, 1974.

Wood Preserving News. This magazine carries frequent articles about pole buildings.

General Building

Anderson, L. O. and Zornig, Harold F. *Build Your Own Low-Cost Home.* New York: Dover Publications, 1972.

Cole, John N. and Wing, Charles. *From the Ground Up.* Boston: Atlantic—Little, Brown Books, 1976. A fine new addition to the library of comprehensive build-it-yourself books. This one introduces simple engineering calculations, and includes much specific, detailed construction information.

Kahn, Lloyd, ed. *Shelter.* Bolinas, California: Shelter Publications, 1973. Distributed by Random House. 175 pages. $6.00. Read this book before you build. Over one thousand pictures illustrate the countless ways, traditional and modern, humans have devised to build houses for themselves. Pole structures abound.

Kern, Ken. *The Owner-Built Home.* New York: Charles Scribner's Sons, 1975. Every new builder should read this classic.

Lytle, R. J. *Farm Builder's Handbook,* 2d ed. Farmington, Michigan: Structures Publishing Co., 1973.

Rapoport, Amos. *House Form and Culture.* Englewood Cliffs, New Jersey: Prentice-Hall, Inc., 1969. An anthropological perspective on traditions of dwelling form.

Roberts, Rex. *Your Engineered House.* New York: M. Evans & Co., 1964. Though occasionally over-specific or outdated, still a fine source of inspiration and ideas for the owner/builder.

Teco Manufacturing Co. *Teco Design Manual.* Teco, 5530 Wisconsin Avenue, Washington D.C. 20015. Teco manufactures metal fastening devices for joining wood members in framing.

United States Department of Agriculture—Forest Service. *Low-Cost Wood Homes For Rural America—Construction Manual.* Washington, D.C.: U. S. Government Printing Office, 1969. 112 pages. Send $1.45 to Superintendent of Documents, USGPO, Washington, D. C. 20402. Ask for Agriculture Handbook No. 364. An excellent, comprehensive and fully illustrated guide to low-cost standard construction methods, with a complete explanation of platform-type pole foundations.

USDA, Forest Service. *Wood-Frame House Construction.* 1976, 222 pages. Send $3.40 to Superintendent of Documents, USGPO. Ask for Agriculture Handbook No. 73. A more elaborate version of the above-listed book, including more options for various building details and components.

USDA. *House Construction—How to Reduce Costs.* 16 pages. Send 50 cents to Superintendent of Documents, USGPO. Ask for Home & Garden Bulletin No. 168. A pamphlet giving rules-of-thumb for reducing building costs.

Plumbing & Electricity

Manas, Vincent T. *National Plumbing Code Illustrated.* St. Petersburg, Florida: Manas Publications, 1968. 240 pages, $8.50. Manas Publications, Shore Tower #205, 1868 Shore Drive South, St. Petersburg, Florida 33707. Manas, a licensed plumber and registered engineer, explains the latest Plumbing Code, supplemented with diagrams and tables.

McGuiness, William J. and Stein, Benjamin. *Mechanical and Electrical Equipment for Buildings,* fifth edition. New York: John Wiley and Sons, Inc., 1971. 1000 pages, $28.95. Available in libraries. A technical textbook for architecture students, this book covers the topics of Basic Electricity, Conductors and Raceways, Service and Utilization Equipment, Wiring Design, and Electric Space Heating in detail. Plumbing topics include Water Systems, Principles of Sanitary Drainage, Plumbing Systems, and Treatment of Sewage and Industrial Wastes. Though residential construction is considered, the emphasis of this book is on larger buildings.

Richter, H. P. *Wiring Simplified.* St. Paul, Minnesota: Park Publishing, 1974. 160 pages, $1.39. Park Publishing, Inc., 1999 Shepard Road, St. Paul, Minn. 55116. Like the Manas book described above, this handbook is a thorough illustrated guide to the National Electrical Code. An excellent buy.

Simplified Electrical Wiring. Sears, Roebuck and Co., 1974. 54 pages, 50 cents. At the other end of the scale, this little booklet tells you how to wire a house, with plenty of illustrations and simplified explanations. Buy it if electricity scares you; you will be cured.

Energy & Conservation

Adams, Anthony. *Your Energy-Efficient House.* Charlotte, Vermont: Garden Way Publishing, 1976. 118 pages, $4.95. Building and remodeling ideas which can drastically reduce fuel bills. Emphasizes natural heating and cooling techniques which use ventilation and insulation to best advantage.

McGuigan, Dermot. *Harnessing the Wind for Home Energy.* Charlotte, Vermont: Garden Way Publishing, 1978. 132 pages, $4.95. A valuable little book, stuffed with information especially valuable to those just getting started with wind power. Plenty of resource and product information.

McGuigan, Dermot. *Harnessing Water Power for Home Energy.* Charlotte, Vermont: Garden Way Publishing, 1978. 100 pages, $4.95. Very complete, readable and up-to-date guide to buying and installing a hydropower system.

Wolfe, Ralph and Clegg, Peter. *Home Energy for the Eighties.* Charlotte, Vermont: Garden Way Publishing, 1979. 300 pages, $10.95. A builder's and owner's encyclopedia of alternative energy sources for the home. Each section (Energy Conservation, Solar Power, Wind Power, Water Power, and Wood Heat) includes a complete catalog of available equipment and hardware, along with a thorough explanation of how to design, choose and install the systems.

AWPI Publications

For information about the uses and characteristics of pressure-treated wood, e.g., poles, piles, patio decks, boat docks, marine bulkheads, and retaining walls, send your request for a list of available publications with a self-addressed, stamped envelope, to the American Wood Preservers Institute (AWPI), 1651 Old Meadow Road, McLean, VA 22102.

This educational arm of the pressure-treated wood industry has available a variety of literature—most at a nominal charge, normally required in advance—to assist the consumer in the proper selection and specification of that industry's products. Some, including design-guide manuals, are quite technical in nature.

Appendix 3

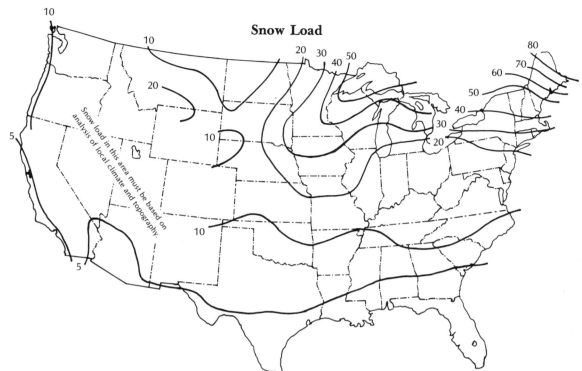

Snow Load

Snow load in psf on the ground, 50-year mean recurrence interval.

Source: U.S. Weather Bureau, Washington, D.C.

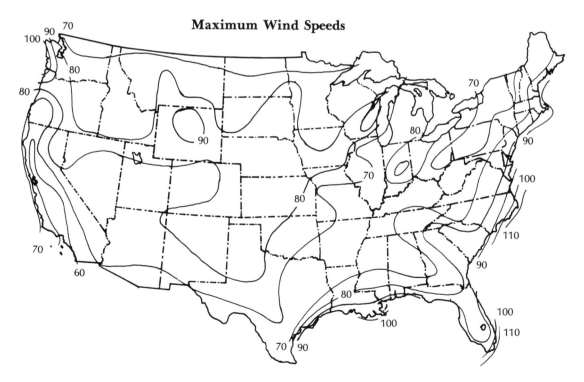

Maximum Wind Speeds

Maximum wind speeds that can be expected to occur once every fifty years.

Index

Other Garden Way Books You Will Enjoy

Award-Winning Passive Solar House Designs, by Jeffrey Cook. Innovative designs incorporating the latest technology. 176 pages, 8½ × 11, 200 illustrations and photos, quality paperback, $14.95.

Build Your Own Low-Cost Log Home, by Roger Hard. Complete log home construction book, step-by-step instructions and diagrams. 204 pages, 8½ × 11, 100 illustrations and photos, quality paperback, $9.95.

Building Small Barns, Sheds and Shelters, by Monte Burch. Construction basics plus plans and how-to instructions for 22 projects. 236 pages, 8½ × 11, 150 illustrations, quality paperback, $12.95.

Homemade: 101 Easy-To-Make Things For Your Garden, Home, Or Farm, by Ken Braren and Roger Griffith. Plans and instructions for making fences, chairs, birdhouses, and dozens of other easy projects for good country living. 176 pages, 8½ × 11, 150 drawings, quality paperback, $6.95.

Timber Frame Construction: All About Post-and-Beam Building, by Jack Sobon and Roger Schroeder. How to design and build, using post-and-beam methods. 208 pages, 8½ × 11, photos and detailed drawings, quality paperback, $12.95.

Solar Projects for Under $500, by Mary Twitchell. Twenty-four low cost passive solar projects, with complete step-by-step instructions and illustrations. 176 pages, 8½ × 11, heavily illustrated, quality paperback, $11.95.

These books are available at your bookstore, lawn and garden center or may be ordered from Garden Way Publishing, Dept. 4412, Schoolhouse Road, Pownal, VT 05261. Please include $1.75 for postage and handling. Send for your free mail order catalog.